THE NO B.S. GUIDE TO MARKETING TO LEADING EDGE BOOMERS & SENIORS

BY

DAN S. KENNEDY
WITH CHIP KESSLER

WITH SPECIAL GUEST CONTRIBUTORS

JEFF GIAGNOCAVO & BEN McCLURE
GARDENER'S MATTRESS

DEAN KILLINGBECK
WWW.NEWCUSTOMERSNOWMARKETING.COM

CHARLES MARTIN, DDS

JULIEANNE E. STEINBACHER & ANDRIANNE J. STAHL
ATTORNEYS AT LAW

Ep
Entrepreneur
PRESS®

Publisher: Entrepreneur Press
Cover Design: Andrew Welyczko
Production and Composition: Eliot House Productions

Library of Congress Cataloging-in-Publication Data
Kennedy, Dan S., 1954–
No B.S. guide to marketing to boomers and seniors: the ultimate no holds barred, take no prisoners roadmap to the money/by Dan S. Kennedy and Chip Kessler.
p. cm.
ISBN-10: 1-59918-450-8 (alk. paper)
ISBN-13: 978-1-59918-450-0 (alk. paper)
1. Older consumers. 2. Consumer behavior. 3. Marketing. I. Kessler, Chip. II. Title.
HF5415.332.O43K46 2012
658.8'343—dc23 2012024914

Printed in the United States of America

17 16 15 14 13 10 9 8 7 6 5 4 3 2 1

"What's it say, Margaret? I'm still not used to these bifocals."

Contents

SECTION 4

RESOURCES

Preface

Dan Kennedy

It's a simple thing.

An expensive, elegant gift from a client. A good-sized, yet compact, magnifying glass, with anodized steel frame, black, soft leather, fold-out handle, and a tiny button that makes it light up.

It is not entirely welcome. Appreciated but not welcome. I don't imagine it a gift anyone really wants, because it is a reminder of age. Oh, I've needed glasses since I was a child, as many people do. But the difficulty of reading what I now think of as impossibly small print that I once thought others' grousing about embarrassing, well, this is a revolting development! The light-up magnifying glass is a bitter pill. Even a well-lit glimpse at mortality. There is no way to replace bulb or battery, perhaps on the assumption that the bulb and battery will outlive me. The little brochure accompanying the glass says the LED bulb will last 10,000 hours. I am not reassured by this. I take it personally.

These are the kind of thoughts a leading-edge boomer or senior has, although he usually keeps them private.

This book is rich in research and well-stocked with examples of astute advertisers, marketers, merchants, and professionals selling to boomers and seniors. The established ruling class of experts in this subject has focused on big corporations, where big money flows to thought leaders and researchers and trend wizards. I've chosen to stay with my small-business compatriots.

And this book is not just research and case histories. Just as with the little magnifying glass, this work was, for me, personal. I am a boomer with senior in sight. In many ways, a classic one. I am growing anxious and irritable, resistant to disruptions to my preferred way of living, reaching backward to nostalgia rather than leaning forward to the unfamiliar, resentful of being thought "out of it," but not eager to be "in it," increasingly concerned with security, safety, and convenience. I am able to indulge my preferences, as I have grown modestly rich, from scratch, entirely through my efforts (like many affluent boomers). So, for example, I have, and in random rotation drive, three classic automobiles including a Rolls-Royce convertible previously owned by Dean Martin that I bought precisely because it was previously owned by Dean Martin.

I am far from the rocking chair: I own a stable of Standardbred racehorses and even drive in 200+ harness races a year myself, professionally competing with drivers who do nothing but that for a living, akin to the late actor Paul Newman becoming a respected professional auto racing driver late in his life. But unlike Paul, I have arranged to live a short distance from the home racetrack. I prefer Florida for vacation, and am considering it for retirement, the traditional migratory path of Ohioans. I am married, many years. We have two homes, adult children, grandchildren, and a dog, over which we both dote and worry.

As we progress through this book, looking closely at leading-edge boomers and seniors, I'll be seeing myself in many places. I bring all this to this book. ***I know how <u>I</u> want to be sold to.*** Rather than taking a from-on-high academic approach, I'm quite willing to display my own biases, preferences, foibles, and frustrations. If you can figure out how to successfully sell to me and satisfy me as a customer, you can open the vault to all the boomer and senior gold, and as you'll learn, there's a lot of it.

The other thing I bring: I know how to sell, and I know how to sell to these customers. Not as a research-driven, theoretical exercise, conducted in corporate environs, in plush conference rooms in Madison Avenue ad agencies and boardrooms in skyscrapers high in the clouds, but down on Main Street, in dentists' offices, in retail shops, in restaurants, in auto repair facilities, in financial advisors' "free workshops." Facing the leading-edge boomer business owner across his well-battered, stacks-cluttered desk. Or, with the boomer couple at their kitchen table. Literally, physically, and through every direct marketing media: mail (the best), print magazines and newspapers, radio, TV, online media.

In my very hands-on consulting and copywriting, I rarely work with the big, brand-name financial services corporation; I work with a group of the financial advisors on their small businesses, on their local advertising and marketing, on their selling. I rarely work with the giant pharmaceutical companies or big hospitals. I work with groups of chiropractors, dentists, and hearing-aid dispensers in their small businesses, their local advertising and marketing, and their selling. My co-author here, Chip Kessler, is much the same; his clients in the elder care, nursing home, and assisted-living industries are predominately small businesses. We live where you likely live.

I have been at this, very successfully—"this" being increasing sales for small businesses—for just a tiny tick shy of 40 years. Over time, I've built a global network of leading marketing consultants in more than 200 different product, service, and profession categories, and through them, along with the entrepreneurs' association built around me, GKIC, I directly influence more than one million business owners annually. My co-author, Chip Kessler, is one of those niche consultants, working inside one particular industry. He is its go-to guy for marketing that works, and I have built a reputation, because I have a time-proven, practical approach that works. We've gotten our hands dirty doing it, and we still do. You can trust this book as real, not theoretical.

Small business has been confronted with some very tough challenges in these recent years. Money stopped pouring out of idiotically appreciating real estate and running uphill right around 2008. As I write this, the full emergence of the New Economy is still delayed, tortured, and impeded by government interference, mismanagement, and malfeasance. **It is critical to go where the money is. To make your business *for* those with money and the willingness to spend it. Meandering round, you'll either starve or be run over. This book is your GPS to the money**. It's as crass as that. It is not a book about social good or business excellence or broad, big, sweeping ideas. It is a manual about getting money from those who have it and are, given reason and their interests met, very willing to spend it. (That, as much as anything, distinguishes today's seniors from previous generations of seniors. The prior group stopped spending and obsessed with turning as much as possible over to their kids and grandkids. This group is not so obsessed. Many reject the idea altogether, from the very rich, like Buffett and Gates, to the ordinary millionaire, even to the retired blue-collar worker. T-shirts emblazoned with "I'm Spending My Kids' Inheritance" are popular items in cruise ship gift shops.)

Even in the worst economy, there is money to be gotten in exchange for goods and services, pinpoint targeted and well-marketed. The most barren and brutal desert has cacti, forbidding perhaps because of their thorny spikes, but full of life-giving water. So what if it is a barren economy? There *are* cacti. There *is* water.

In an improving, re-awakening economy, this time around, it is the boomers and seniors who are and will be the chief spenders.

This book is, therefore, an opportunity manual. Don't just read it. Use it. Work with it. If you are a leading-edge boomer like me, or a senior, you know what that word means: work.

Oh, and just for the record, I don't really *need* the damn magnifying glass. It's just a nice desk decoration. Or the perfect item to re-gift. (Boomers invented re-gifting.)

Editorial Notes:

- Throughout the book, we will be referring to leading-edge boomers—i.e., age 58 to 66—and seniors as LEB/S.
- No attempt has been made at politically correct gracefulness, evening out "he" and "she" or constantly saying "she and he" and "he and she." We aren't getting paid by the word. You'll find "he" used throughout as convenience, not as slight.

SECTION 1

WHO ARE THESE PEOPLE?

CHAPTER 1

Meet the LEB/S Market

Dan Kennedy

Americans born between 1946 and 1964 number nearly 80 million and make up about 26% of the U.S. population. Roughly one in four consumers is a boomer. Obviously, these boomers will become seniors, thus "the age wave" will dominate this economy and this marketplace for many years to come. Every day, for the next 18 years, 8,000 to 10,000 boomers will reach age 65. In each of those years, about 3 million.

Younger boomers, age 48 to 57, exhibit significantly different attitudes and behaviors than do older, or leading-edge, boomers, age 58 to 66. This book focuses on the leading-edge boomers, hereinafter referred to as LE-boomers, and on seniors, who have much in common. When no distinction is being made, we'll be referring to them as LEB/S. Mac Brand, partner in Bellwether Food

Group, says, "The lines between seniors and baby boomers are blurring." Jim Gilmartin, founder of Coming of Age Inc., points out that the combined boomer+senior consumer population tops 117 million, "forming the largest economic group in America, with annual spending power of more than $2 trillion."

What do LEB/S consumers buy? Just about everything, and more of it, at higher average prices than any other consumers. Averaged from research from multiple sources, here are my own numbers, rounded off, in some example categories (percentage of total revenues of the category):

Home Furnishings	55%
Luxury Real Estate	70%
Support of the Arts	60%
Mail-Order Catalogs	75%
Luxury Travel	80%
Charitable Donations	65%
Women's Apparel	50%

Oddly, despite LEB/S accounting for more than half the sales in just about every product and service category, advertising, marketing, and often even product development is still weighted heavily toward other target demographics. This may reflect some strategic thinking; worry about dependency on customers dying off. It more likely reflects companies turning over these decisions to young and even very young people who have little interest in or respect for these consumers.

It is generally true: As restaurants go, so goes the economy. U.S. restaurant industry growth is predicted to fall short of a miserly 1% a year through 2019, not even keeping pace with population growth, according to the "Future of Foodservice Study" reported in *Nation's Restaurant News*. The reason for the near zero growth is the dominance of the LEB/S population. As they grow older, they dine out less, they spend less when they do dine out, and they have different interests in dining. The chief author of the study, Bonnie Riggs, says that "the big competitor is the home. They find it not only cheaper to eat at home, but they believe it tastes better, they can do it more leisurely, and they can eat healthier at home."

My own take on this adds a fourth factor, I think grossly underestimated by the restaurant industry, and a central key to success with LEB/S presented by this book: **Restaurants' delivery of one generic experience for all age groups is unappealing, and is more than enough to tip the scales in favor of "Let's just stay home *and avoid the aggravation.*"** LEB/S prefer a relatively quiet, orderly dining experience, so being seated near a family with young children, placed in a noisy environment, hemmed into too-tight quarters, being asked to stand around waiting for a table (holding *a device* that summons them when a table becomes available), feeling hurried at their table, even having a young wait staff that is impatient or ill-informed all serve up a dissatisfying experience. The answer is in the overarching premise of this book: If you want the LEB/S consumers, you are going to have to create and deliver an experience matched with their preferences, or at minimum, one absent factors they find annoying and off-putting.

It's Complicated

The LEB/S population is far from one homogeneous group. It contains leading-edge boomers in second, third, etc., marriages, many with younger partners, some starting second families, but also empty-nesters and re-nesters with adult children moving back in—sometimes with their young kids in tow—caregivers taking on responsibility for adult parents, retirees, widows and widowers, healthy and active, ill and infirm, rich and poor. As you proceed through this book, you'll find different chapters devoted to different kinds of LEB/S and to different issues, i.e., buying motives, in their lives. One key point from this: Few businesses can treat LEB/S as a single market with one-size-fits-all products and services, advertising and marketing. Instead, most need to select a segment or segments within LEB/S to focus on.

With regard to money and spending power, one of the leading consumer research organizations, Pew, found boomers to be the age group most likely to say they took significant losses on investments during the recession, beginning in 2008. Sixty percent of the LE-boomers said they might need to postpone planned retirement. Even relatively affluent LE-boomers have significant concerns about losses suffered during the recession, from investments or income budgeted to go to retirement savings. A survey of millionaires for the Centurion Group of financial advisors found that the number-one worry of over 60% was overspending, thus running out of money with too many years left on the clock. Still, over half the nation's wealth and more of its discretionary spending power is in the hands of LEB/S.

Convergence of LEB/S and Affluent Consumers

When I wrote the first edition of the book *No B.S. Marketing to the Affluent* in 2008, I made much of the concentration of both wealth and discretionary spending power into the hands of the LEB/S population. What was foreseen and documented then is proving true to the nth degree. Currently, according to the Ipsos Mendelsohn Affluent Generations Study (ipsos.com), four in ten affluents are boomers—households with median income of $140,000.00, although the income alone is deceiving, as 46% of this group have net worths exceeding $2 million. This puts the affluent boomers at about 25 million. Another 9% of U.S. affluence is in the hands of seniors, putting the combined LEB/S control of the money in the 50% neighborhood. To say it another way, simply, one out of every two dollars available to advertisers, marketers, merchants, and service providers is in the wallets of LEB/S.

LEB/S spending varies widely. The more affluent LEB/S, as the CEO of AgeWave.com, Dr. Ken Dychtwald, puts it, make "the psychological shift from acquiring more material possessions to *a desire to purchase* enjoyable, satisfying, and memorable experiences." Good news for marketers: They are not *stopping* spending as previous generations of seniors did. Not even spending that reluctantly. Just spending differently for different reasons.

Resource

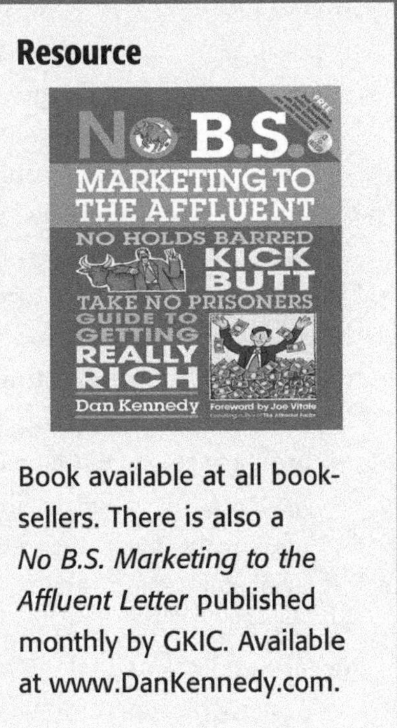

Book available at all booksellers. There is also a *No B.S. Marketing to the Affluent Letter* published monthly by GKIC. Available at www.DanKennedy.com.

Younger boomers as well as some LE-boomers have been trading down during the recession, when, in the past, this would have been a group almost exclusively making upward mobility purchases, trading up in most categories. A company like McDonald's has been seen attempting to capitalize on this trend with its McCafé specialty coffees and beverages—an open invitation to Starbucks' customers.

The New Senior

For the New Senior, classic or traditional age-defined attitudes and behaviors are pushed further along in years. Jim Gilmartin, founder of Coming of Age Inc., a marketing agency specializing in the LEB/S market, cautions against using traditional descriptive language. "Be careful what you call them. Euphemisms like 'elder' or 'of a certain age' may not go over well. Many have become upset with being labeled."

This population of seniors is fighting age more than any previous generation, refusing to go quietly into the good night. It has paraded out the "60 is the new 40," now "70 is the new 50" lines, a statement of aspiration if not determined intent. In the skin-care products industry, where I do some consulting and advertising copywriting work, we see the average age of the consumer creeping up. One company selling anti-wrinkle potions has seen its average buyer age move from 57 to 69 in just five years, and further, is finding the older buyer group easier to close on the incoming calls, i.e., delivering a better prospect-to-buyer conversion rate and lower cost per sale, and exhibiting less price resistance. Parallel changes are occurring in cosmetic surgery and cosmetic dentistry.

A big aspiration among LEB/S is quality of life, not just longevity. Seniors are living longer, and are healthy for more years, ill and infirm for fewer years, than in previous generations. The health-care industry's term for this is "compression of morbidity." For a wide spectrum of businesses, this means two things: First, there is greater long-term or lifetime customer value in relationships with LEB/S consumers than there would have been a generation ago, so catering to them makes better business sense than ever before. Second, seniors will remain mobile and actively interested longer in products, services, and experiences that they have historically deserted at age 65.

An Assortment of Facts

How LEB/S *think*—that's the real key to successfully marketing to them. This quick list from the "2010 Del Webb Baby Boomer Survey" conducted by Del Webb, the owner and developer of many retirement communities, offers insight into how they think about themselves . . .

- Boomers set the benchmark of "old age" at—hold your breath—80.
- There is considerable distance between their chronological age and the age they identify with, which is 15 years younger. That has profound bearing on photos and images placed in advertising, the age and appearance of actors or celebrities used in commercials, language used by copywriters. Make a big note of this.
- More than 50% of boomers say they exercise regularly, and feel they are in better shape than they were some years ago.
- Trailing-edge boomers believe they need to accumulate more savings than LE-boomers. Nearly half are skeptical of government benefits being available when they become seniors.
- 72% of boomers intend to keep working past the classic retirement age of 65.
- In their thinking about retirement migration, a warm and sunny climate is not the chief magnet as it has long been for generations of seniors. Instead, cost of living, and access to health care are more important.

How Will You Prosper Embracing the Opportunities Presented by the LEB/S Markets?

This book is not an exhaustive and comprehensive examination. I'm not even sure such a thing is possible. Successfully marketing to LEB/S is more a multilayered project than a subject. Our primary purpose here is to be *provocative*: to get you thinking about where you fit in, what opportunities may exist and be best for you, so that you can define your own path forward and then get to work, including gathering the specific information you need, probably from a myriad of sources. In the Resources section beginning on page 264, I have listed all the sources we secured information from, the most informative websites, and the experts devoted to the LEB/S market as their sole work.

Whether you are left out of the Age/Profit Wave, merely get small benefit by accident, by just being there, or develop a well-organized strategy to mine riches from different segments of this consumer population depends on you and what you do.

After I wrote the first edition of the *No B.S. Marketing to the Affluent* book in 2008, it became clear that couldn't be "done" in a single book either, but it was more an ongoing project. On my end, it begat a series of small group summits, one of which is available in product form now at www.DanKennedy.com/store, and a continuing monthly *No B.S. Marketing to the Affluent Letter.* It led to the book in the No B.S. series immediately preceding this one, *No B.S. Guide to Trust-Based Marketing,* which grew out of intimate work with financial advisors, health-care professionals, and others marketing to affluent LEB/S clients. That led to this. It is all an interconnected work in progress. When Einstein was asked how he made his breakthrough scientific discoveries, he replied, "I grope." There is a tendency to want a simple, 1–2–3 recipe and a set of fill-in-the-blanks templates for marketing to a target audience, but I'm afraid real success can't be put into a single, little box. We're hopeful you'll become as fascinated with the opportunities presented by the Age/Profit Wave as we are, and join us in—groping.

A Note About the Rest of the Wave

The explosive growth and impact on markets of LEB/S is not exclusive to America. Asia has 1.2 billion baby boomers. By 2050, the number of people over age 60 in Asia will exceed that number. The combined segment of that population 50+ now controls 55% of all the consumer spending and 80% of the wealth. There is approximately $11 trillion U.S. under their control. According to the "Investing in Asia Conference's Report," the percentages of spending and wealth will continue to shift to the 50-and-over group in coming years. Europe offers a similar situation. While this book is U.S.-focused with its specific information, the overarching strategies apply anywhere there is spending power and net worth concentrated in the hands of LEB/S.

CHAPTER 2

LEB/S in the Workforce

Chip Kessler

Go into a McDonald's these days, and where there used to be only pimply-faced teenagers staring at you from across the counter you now often find a man or woman old enough to be your father or mother or even grandfather or grandmother. In the past, the fast-food industry's jobs were for high school kids who wanted extra money, college kids working their way through school, or young adults not going to college. It was and is a career path for some, moving up to store manager, area manager, executive. But somebody's grandparent? The first few times I saw it, I found it unsettling. My first thought was boredom escape for retirees. Adult day care plus extra spending money. It took a bit for the thought to settle in, that this person might need this job and its paycheck. What this person did for 30 or 40 years had not left them well enough off financially. Forced into early retirement. Wounded by bad investments. Not somebody trying to pass the time—somebody who wanted to afford three meals a day on a regular basis!

The senior employee in need of a low-level job is not exclusively found in the fast-food workforce. Your average Walmart greeter and many cashiers in various stores can remember when Superman made his debut in *Action Comics* in 1938, and voted for either Truman or Dewey in 1948. If you travel, you bump into more and more seniors driving cabs and airport shuttle buses.

There are even rich and famous LEB/S who arrive at their 60s or 70s with very little left of very large incomes that passed through their hands. Arnold Schwarzenegger, Clint Eastwood, and Burt Reynolds are all LEB/S peers. Two are wealthy, one is broke. If it's true of the famous, it's true of the un-famous. The gray-haired clerk at the Ace Hardware store may have been a six-figure-income executive a few years back.

The fast-growing graying workforce is complex with contradictions within. According to the U.S. Bureau of Labor Statistics, the number of Americans age 55 and older continuing to work is projected to grow 3.3% by 2020, **making up as much as 25% of the U.S. workforce**, up from just 13% in 2010, nearly **a 200% increase** over the decade. This puts more seniors in the workforce than at any time in nearly 40 years.

There's a gender bias: Labor force participation by women age 55 and older has grown significantly in the past two decades, from just 23% in 1990 to 35% in 2010, and nearly four in ten, 40%, are expected to be working in 2020. Interestingly, participation in work by women age 16 to 24 is declining; 63% were in the workforce in 2000, only 53% in 2010, and only 45% are projected to be at work in 2020.

You can look at this largely as a natural byproduct of the LEB/S population living longer and therefore choosing to delay retirement and continue working longer, and of women outliving men, it being easier for older women to land jobs than older men, and women being willing to take jobs that men won't. It is, in some ways, a reflection of "70 is the new 50"—making 85 the new 65. There is also an economic need factor at play. And pretty much unsaid publicly, a growing employer preference for the more reliable and responsible older employee.

In a front-page story in *USA Today* (4/5/12), "Most Jobs Go to Older Workers," it was reported that in February 2012, employment for LEB/S rose by 277,000, taking 65% of the total job gains. That article attributes the LEB/S staying in and returning to the workforce to the recession, pension insecurity and changes, longevity, and even unexpected financial need suddenly landed in LEB/S laps: the need to support their unemployed adult children. The irony of the senior behind the counter at McDonald's because of a need to give financial aid to his 27-year-old unemployed college graduate is mind-boggling.

On the other hand, LEB/S exiting the workforce has impact, too. In the months I was doing most of the work on this chapter, in mid-2012, The U.S. Labor Department attributed the slight drop in the nation's unemployment rate month to month, from 8.2% to 8.1%, to a shrinking labor force—not to any actual economic improvement. The chief economist at Moody's Analytics found that, of the 6.7 million who dropped out of the labor force during the month, 60% were employed (not the unemployed so discouraged they stopped looking for jobs, as politicians liked claiming), and that has been the pattern since 2010. The Moody's analysts believe this partly reflects LEB/S voluntary retirements. Dean Maki, the chief U.S. economist at Barclays Capital, drew from government data that 18.8% of Americans who were not active in the labor force and said they didn't want jobs were 55 and older, up from 17.8% when the recession started, which he says closely tracks the rise in new Social Security recipients. The unknown factor is the crossover between retirement and discouragement in seeking work. In a *USA Today* article at this time, a 67-year-old woman who had lost her job as a full-time minister in 2007 said she finally stopped looking for full-time work and officially retired in 2009 because she had grown weary of being rejected and disappointed. That's hardly voluntary retirement. My own idea about this is that the crossover factor is huge, and should there be significant economic recovery with job growth, many of the LEB/S retirees will return to the workplace.

Predicting the future is always dicey, but AARP surveys show that the majority of baby boomers predict they will keep working to or past age 70. Forty-one percent said they weren't particularly interested in retirement before then, and 36% said they would NEVER be able to afford to fully retire.

Of course, companies have been and continue to shrink or freeze growth of workforces in the U.S., and re-allocate capital to creating jobs beyond U.S. borders—true of everybody from Apple, to a handful of fast-food franchisors, to a number of retailers. Government jobs have ballooned under the Obama administration, but one can foresee a wave of austerity around the corner. An increasing number of LEB/S workers will be pushed to early retirement. In May 2012, the financially troubled U.S. Postal Service offered $15,000.00 in early retirement incentives to 45,000 mail sorters. This likelihood of continued job shrinkage juxtaposed with the already high unemployment rate and the desire of the majority of LEB/S to stay in the workforce to age 70 does not paint a pretty picture. It even sets up an age war for available jobs!

Self-employment is another matter altogether.

Many business owners are remaining at the helm longer than hoped or anticipated, for both financial and emotional reasons. The dried-up financing of recent years has made it much harder for small-business owners to sell their businesses, particularly to promising young employees, unless willing to be the bank and thus at risk rather than retired with financial security in place. A client of Dan Kennedy's, Dr. Greg Stanley, CEO of Whitehall

Management, a leading business and financial consultancy to thousands of dentists, says that the sale of the practice to younger dentists stopped serving as the preferred exit strategy as the Bernanke policies brought yields on safe, fixed-income investments to near zero, coupled with a threat of significant inflation at some point. The dentist selling the practice lacks good options for converting that cash into sufficient passive income to retire as intended. Instead, Stanley's team is guiding dentists in retaining ownership and management of their practices with the patient care entirely delivered by associate doctors, a form of "non-retirement retirement."

Generational business succession in the small-business community is also at an all-time low, so the traditional passage of many kinds of businesses—notably including agricultural, small manufacturing, and retail—to sons and daughters is unavailable, compelling the owners to stay in place into their 60s, 70s, and even their 80s.

There is also a trend of LEB/S "third-act entrepreneurship," some motivated by financial need, some motivated by disinterest in or boredom with traditional retirement. The percentage of business owners age 55 to 65 selling their businesses and starting new businesses, buying outright or buying into businesses, or creating consulting businesses with significant revenues within 6 to 18 months of the original business' sale has nearly doubled over the past 10 years, according to our own research, utilizing U.S. government statistics, franchise industry statistics, and other cobbled-together data. Some franchisors have specifically targeted this group, such as the BurgerFi chain, which began advertising in affluent-oriented media like private jet travel magazines, specifically promoting their business as ideal for the already successful and prosperous individual who recently sold a business or retired "young" from a career. Dan Kennedy has a number of clients in what he calls low-barrier-to-entry entrepreneurship, offering pre-packaged opportunities or comprehensive training in starting small, homebased businesses, "kitchen table" e-commerce and mail-order businesses, independent real estate investing, and consulting and coaching, and with virtually all of them the interest from the LEB/S population is steadily growing. In some cases, they are now repositioning their opportunities and their advertising to target and specifically appeal to this group. Kennedy anticipates a booming industry entirely devoted to supporting LEB/S new/third-act entrepreneurs, with businesses that offer considerable work-schedule flexibility, low-risk, low-permanent investment, and interesting activity. A growing number of LEB/S entrepreneurs will not want to be ankle-chained to a brick-and-mortar location and rigid schedule, but will want interesting, rewarding work to do, and good opportunity to earn income.

One of the leading experts in marketing to LEB/S, Mary Furlong, author of the book *Turning Silver into Gold: How to Profit in the New Boomer Marketplace,* agrees: "Most boomers intend to work all their lives, but few boomers who keep working will settle for just any job. Millions of them seek creativity and passion in their work lives. They are more likely than previous generations to want work that reflects their values and identity. They want to make a difference and have fun while doing it." Well, where better can they exercise this sort of preference control over their work than through self-employment?

Businesses that Kennedy has connection with, actively engaged in bringing forward LEB/S-appropriate self-employment opportunities that you might find interesting to examine include www.safetytechnology.com and www.awaionline.com, the home of American Writers & Artists, where novices can learn at an accelerated pace to become freelance article writers, travel writers, and advertising copywriters. GKIC, the association of entrepreneurs built around Dan, coupled with Dan's leadership, facilitates the startup of thousands of businesses in diverse product and service categories every year, a growing number by LEB/S. See page 264 for more information about GKIC.

What Does the Workplace Age Wave Mean to Marketers?

It's important not to think of age and retirement in historical, traditional terms. At one point, 65 was the magic number, and everyone arriving could be thought of as merrily strolling off to Florida and Arizona, to shuffleboard and canasta games and early bird buffets, and marketers could either ignore them, or easily generalize offerings for them.

With upwards of 50% remaining at work, re-entering work after years away, holding onto businesses longer, and starting new businesses, the matinee movie and its equivalents in countless categories promises to have a shrinking audience.

Under these circumstances, diverse product and service needs and desires are matched with later and later ages. You've seen the TV ads for the elevator chair to be installed at home, so climbing stairs is replaced with the safer alternative—but that guy now has to commute to a workplace every day! Both he and his employer have needs. These senior workers will keep spending, but spend very differently than their fathers did at 65.

It's also important to keep in mind that LEB/S do not sit in the same financial boat. There's a whole fleet, from little, leaky rowboats to grandiose yachts. There are moneyed LEB/S still working or still in business. Presidential candidate Romney is one. As Dan wrote in an issue of his *No B.S. Marketing to the Affluent Letter*: "Talking to Romney about the lower maintenance costs of one automobile versus another telegraphs to him that you aren't the guy he should be doing business with. He lives with a surprising number of others in the 'if you have to ask the price, it's not for you' universe." These successful, prosperous LEB/S still working by choice, not need, can obviously be very valuable customers or clients. They are busy, may have diminishing capacity to do all sorts of things, and have money to pay and the willingness to pay to have more things done for them than ever before in their lives: Their homes kept up for them; their meals prepared for them; a driver or car service on demand; even a personal aide at their side throughout their business day. I'm wondering about my own industry: Will there be seniors running their companies or going to work every day who'll want to return to the safety, security, and convenience of upscale assisted living centers at night? These facilities may soon be about more than serving rather infirm or family-less seniors tucked away to retirement.

Super-creative, capable, and successful people are usually reluctant to quit despite age. Consider all those in the public eye who've retired then regretted it and come back. Boomer Jay Leno's retirement from *The Tonight Show* was very short-lived. Back in the 1970s Frank Sinatra once briefly retired, but came roaring back after a year. What has Jack Welch's retirement from GE looked like? Writing books, taking speaking engagements, serving on corporate boards, consulting, even becoming a business media personality, frequently appearing on the CNBC and Fox Financial networks. My colleague Dan Kennedy has nearly retired at two different times, even running a series of "last ever" seminars on different subjects, followed by a retirement party complete with comedy roast. It appears to most of us he is working as much or more than at any time—and why not, when he's at the top of his game, can sell out venues as a speaker, and is in high demand as a consultant? Look at Joan Rivers, a very senior celebrity and entrepreneur, and boomer Gene Simmons, both of whom have appeared with Dan at GKIC SuperConferences℠ in recent years. Both have TV shows and business enterprises, and tour; both often work 10-to-12 hour days; both are taking on new opportunities despite absence of any financial motivation for doing so. For every such visible LEB/S hyperactive entrepreneur or creative type, there must be thousands under the radar, in communities all across America. This group needs and will need increasing amounts and diversity of support to continue as they are.

There are also the needy LEB/S, continuing to work and juggle the expenses of apparel, transportation, etc., related to being in the workforce with household expenses, against a limited, fixed income. Many, as described in another chapter, also have adult children who moved back "home." This makes them older versions of the working parent, with many of the same needs for goods and services and desire for an occasional break from the stress and routine as working parents and heads of households half their age!

There are still retirees, early, on-schedule, and late. Retired, financially well off, spending on lifestyle. Retired, financially secure, spending more carefully, on a smaller range of products, services, and experiences. Retired, financially restricted, spending on basics and necessities. Retired, in financial difficulty—losing homes, cashing out annuities and insurance policies, selling family heirlooms via eBay, Craigslist, and swap meets.

Trying to make room in a business's product, price, and marketing strategies for all these different LEB/S folks is far more difficult than it was to make room for the age 65 and over customers when they all shifted needs, interests, and buying behavior in unison. Neither the boomer nor LEB/S population can be lumped together and fed the same products, services, prices, or advertising messages.

In my own work consulting with nursing home and assisted living operators (www.ExtendedCareProducts.com), I'm not only confronted with the challenge of marketing to LEB/S, but also having to communicate with LE-boomers making preparatory investigations and purchases for themselves, LE-boomers making decisions involving a spouse—perhaps the older of the two in the marriage—LE-boomers making decisions for an elderly parent, seniors making decisions for themselves, and seniors making decisions involving a spouse. My signature consumer outreach, which can be seen at www.ChoicesForCare.com, uses a dual/multiple-path approach to promote my Discovery Program on the range of care-giving options to the general public. Because it is broad marketing, it has to simultaneously speak to people interested on their own behalf and people taking on responsibility for assisting or making decisions for others, and has to cover nursing home, assisted living, retirement community, adult day care service, and at-home healthcare alternatives. That's a lot of holes to dig and places to have to dig holes with just one shovel!

Whenever possible, I prefer guiding my clients in this field to more targeted marketing aimed at more precisely chosen segments of LEB/S, but we also need to be effective with a cast-the-broadest-net approach in order to dominate a market. You may be in the same situation, where having one, big, broad marketing approach is necessary but is not enough.

CHAPTER 3

"Dad, Mom, I'm Home!"

Chip Kessler

What mother doesn't like hearing, "Mom, I'm home!" when their son or daughter bounds merrily through the front door? They're happy to see you. They've had a big day. They're hungry. You may need to scold them because they've left their room a mess once again, but the smile on their face makes you leave it to another time. This happy family scene plays out in homes every day and has done so since the days of black-and-white TV sitcoms. But what if this darling child bounding through the door is 28 instead of 8?

The new economic pressures on LEB/S are remarkable. LEB/S suffered greater investment losses in the big meltdown than any other group. They saw from 15% to 50% of their retirement savings, stock portfolios, and home values erased; now, they're seeing a number of years of nominal to no effective yield on savings. On, say, $500,000.00, the difference between a 4% and a 1% yield is the difference between getting ahead and falling behind. Three percent equals $15,000.00 that was expected but hasn't been there, times the 4 years from 2008 to 2012 equals $60,000.00 missing. In effect, an 8% loss of principal. If that income was planned on and needed, it had to be actually drained from principal. After just 8 years of this, this investor has gone from $500,000.00 to $420,000.00, on which he would need a 5% yield to achieve the income he originally hoped for from 4%.

At the same time, the LEB/S parent has been called on to provide housing, food, and other financial support to their adult offspring, far beyond the normal and customary call of duty. According to the Pew Research Center, nearly 1 in 4 Americans age 18 to 34 have moved back to their parents' homes after living on their own. 1 in 4! Combining the boomerangers and the fast-growing failure-to-launch generation, 39%—nearly 4 in 10 adults in this age group—live under their parents' roof! Remarkably and terrifyingly, the majority self-describe as "well satisfied" with these living arrangements.

Some who have left the nest haven't traveled very far, and the parents are still parenting. According to the "American Express Youth Finance Survey," 57% of adults 19 to 29 years of age are at least partially dependent on their parents to pay their *basic* bills. Eighty percent of these 19- to 29-year-olds self-identify as "feeling overwhelmed with handing their financial situation." According to surveys conducted by VibrantNation.com, nearly 6 in 10 boomer moms pay the cell phone bills for at least one of their adult children! Independence, yes. Self-reliance, no.

A Forbes.com piece presents the following breakdown of where LEB/S spending on adult children is going: 50% housing, 48% living expenses (food, utilities, etc.), 41% transportation costs, 35% insurance, 28% medical, and 29% spending money.

"Hi, Dad. Investment banking wasn't that great after all."

From a marketing standpoint, don't miss that this makes LEB/S buyers and potential buyers of goods and services they might not ordinarily buy for themselves, or potential multibuyers of the same products and services. For example, parents are paying to keep their adult kids on a family plan with the cell phone company, the gym or fitness center, the chiropractic practice, buying maid service for their home and their son's or daughter's home, joining or rejoining Costco given shopping for two households instead of one.

More than half of the boomer women with offspring ages 18 to 34 spend more than $5,000.00 a year subsidizing each of their grown children, so many are shelling out $10,000.00, $15,000.00 and more. Seventeen percent of these moms put the tab at $10,000.00 to $20,000.00 per adult child. There's good reason the most popular known item in President Obama's health insurance reform package was the mandate to insurers to raise the age for adult children remaining on parents' policies to 26 (a cost shared by *all* payers for health insurance, whether employers or individuals. If you have no dependent adult children, but your insurance premiums went up, you're paying for somebody else's 24-year-old dependent.)

Emotional Reasons Fuel Growing Acceptance by Parents of Supporting Adult Offspring

The Forbes.com article quoted a psychologist explaining that baby boomer values make them susceptible to paying more of their adult kids' bills and paying for them longer because "in the last 20 to 30 years, the family structure has become more child-centered. Boomer parents were very willing to make sacrifices for their kids, giving them the sense it would continue until they were on their feet (however long that takes). Now these parents are supporting their adult kids' lifestyles." While many such parents worry that they are permitting their offspring to be too dependent on them, they are extremely reluctant to cut them off. There is even a poll by Harris Interactive, conducted for Forbes Women and The National Endowments for Financial Education, indicating that 26% of parents have taken on new and additional debt because of paying their adult children's bills, and 7% are delaying intended retirement due to this added financial burden. A senior debt bomb may be in the formative stages as an effect of this!

When it comes to forking over cash to adult offspring, not all kids get equal treatment. The *USA Today* article (5/3/12) headlined "Parents Pay and They Play Favorites" outlines stark realities drawn from a University of Michigan study incorporating 2,000 people age 19 to 22 and their LEB/S parents: 62% are receiving parental financial assistance, averaging out to $12,185.00 a year. But the secret is that adult children who displayed certain personality and behavioral traits at young ages are more likely than others to be generously subsidized as adults. Parents admitted that cheerful children who got along well with others during their preteen years are getting more help as adults than those who were "difficult children."

Grandparents have not escaped the upstream movement of financial responsibilities, either. A hotel and travel industry study group has tracked a growing trend of lodging bills for two generations of visitors to the elder's home city or three generations traveling together all being paid by the eldest, i.e., the grandparents. Also, travel by grandparents to visit children and grandchildren in far-flung places vs. being visited by their families has increased steadily over the recession years, in terms of percentages, number and frequency of trips per year, and money spent.

The news of mid-2012 included a great deal of focus on the college debt bomb; the huge numbers of young people graduating or

"Son, your mother and I think that you are now old enough to get your own drink of water."

soon to graduate college with student loan debt in the six-figures coupled with a dismal jobs outlook.

If you factor all this together—the college debt bomb, the nearly jobless recovery from recession, and the lax attitudes about dependency of the 18 to 34 population as well as those immediately behind it, the emotional attitudes of the LEB/S parents—you get a picture of unprecedented financial pressure on LEB/S.

The Squeeze Play

All this, only half their troubles!

There is a squeeze play, too. At the same time there's a tidal wave of adult children moving back home with mom and dad, there's a tidal wave of elderly parents of those same moms and dads hitting the infirmity wall and needing caregivers, and/or the financial insecurity wall, needing financial support.

More than 65 million people, a huge percentage of them LE-boomers, report having to devote 10 to 20 hours a week to care for their parents. This falls more to women than men, and women frequently set aside their careers under pressure of this responsibility.

A Merrill Lynch "Wealth Management Survey" of boomers with investable assets of $250,000.00 or more shows that 31% are now financially supporting BOTH their adult age children and their senior parents.

Net worth, income and time to earn income, and spending power is being drained from those caught in the squeeze play. Forty-five percent say they have made sacrifices in spending for themselves, 44% say they've cut back on luxury spending, 25% say they have stopped saving for their own retirement, 12% have stopped saving for their younger children's college educations, and 20% say they are considering having senior parents or/and adult children move in with them to cut living expenses for all concerned.

When They Flock Together, New Opportunities Arise

None of this means there's *no* money left for you to get from the LEB/S consumers affected in this manner. In some categories, there's more spending done by a single consumer/head of household. In some categories, there are new and different needs born of these new living situations. A client of Dan's in the home remodeling business has enjoyed a multimillion-dollar boom in his business in part driven by LEB/S spending to make their adult parents' homes age safe and functional as an alternative to incurring the cost of placing the senior in a nursing or assisted-living facility, or having a portion of their own home made age functional for their elderly parent moving back in with them. Remodelers also report an uptick in bathroom and kitchenette installations and other remodeling to garages, basements and suites of rooms in homes where adult children are moving back in with their parents with intent of long-term cohabitation. As an anecdotal example, in one family's consolidation, two of four cars were sold and the proceeds used to fund home remodeling. In my industry, encompassing nursing homes and assisted living centers but also home health care, we are going to have to get more creative in the product/service/price options we offer, and continually update our marketing based on these different family units.

Lots of new legal, financial, and family issues arise. People are dealing with tenant and cohabitation agreements for the first time. Obamacare includes the well-publicized provision compelling health insurance companies to permit parents to carry adult children on their policies to age 26, but there are other interesting government forays. New legislation *requires* parents to co-sign for credit cards for children under age 21, unless the 18- to 21-year-old can demonstrate sufficient income to qualify independently, and these co-signers put their own credit scores and credit standing at risk by doing so, potentially risking increased interest rates on their credit cards, reduced access to credit, even increases in insurance premiums (as insurers now utilize credit scores in judging other risks). Over two-thirds of all cell phone plans are now family plans, with the parents carrying the kids into their late 20s and 30s, with full responsibility. Jr. has agreed to reimburse Mom for his share of the bill, but what happens when he doesn't? In some states parents are required to be joint owners of checking accounts until their offspring turn 18, but many fail to undo that embroilment, leaving it alone to capture waived banking fees or other perks tied to balances and usage, but when Jr. overdraws that account or blows up the debit card, who's the bank gonna call? Parents are increasingly asked to co-sign and guarantee apartment and house rental agreements and leases, auto loans, and other obligations for their adult children. After working hard to get their mortgage paid off, they are put back on the hook. And when that adult child abruptly decides to move across the country for a job or romantic attachment, what about the remaining months on the lease or the vacant house?

We're seeing everyone, from famous finance authors and experts like Suze Orman and Dave Ramsey to new, upstart personalities and entities, stepping into advice-giving on these thorny matters and even new life-coaching businesses devoted to helping LEB/S parents get their adult kids out of the house and into gainful employment!

Marketing to "The New Family"

Over time, the snapshot of the American family has changed and keeps changing, and boomers have had a great deal to do with the transformation and diversification. The single parent with children, especially the *intentional* single parent with children, was once such an oddity that an episode of the *Mad Men* show, set in the late '50s, featured an entire neighborhood engaged in gossip and disapproval over the single mother suddenly in their midst. The triple-generation family with one head of household finances and a number of

co-mingled, complex financial entanglements is the newest family scenario, somewhat of boomers' making although not necessarily of boomers' intent or liking.

It's now up to us marketers to recognize it as a new norm, and to craft and present appropriate products, services, and marketing messages.

CHAPTER 4

The Good Ol' Days

Chip Kessler

"They don't make em' like they used to!"

No doubt, you've heard some senior say this to you. He or she may be referring to anything from today's modern automobiles to the piece of apple pie you both got in your favorite neighborhood restaurant. In many instances the person is right. It seems that a day doesn't go by that we're not hearing about some recall for this make of car or that one. As for that piece of apple pie, if you grew up with a mother or grandmother who delighted in baking such delicious treats, chances are the pie you get in a restaurant won't be as mouth-watering.

Here's something else that a senior will also say: Despite all the financial ills of recent years, the recession we've gone through doesn't hold a candle to the Great Depression of the late 1920s and 1930s. And no matter what financial and/or personal setbacks that may have occurred in your life because of the recent woes, the senior is correct—what we've experienced of late doesn't hold a candle to what took place in that terrible period. During that period, *Wikipedia* reports, unemployment in the United States rose to 25%, and in some countries overseas, to as much as 33%. International trade fell by over 50%. Heavy industry nose-dived, farming tanked as crop prices fell by as much as 60%. Banks failed left and right. Think about it: One out of four to as many as one out of three people was out of a job, and it wasn't because some people chose not to work in favor of collecting an unemployment check from the federal government.

Most of us have seen old newsreel footage of the times and/or heard the stories passed on from generation to generation:

- People standing in lines several blocks long waiting to buy a loaf of bread.
- Men who were financially successful one moment jumping from rooftops because their fortunes were wiped out in the Stock Market Crash of October 29, 1929.
- Hundreds and hundreds of able-bodied men applying for only a handful of jobs.

Imagine if you lived through this as a teenager or younger child. Maybe you were a young adult, full of vim and vigor, ready to tackle the world and make your mark, only to have your legs pulled out from under you. Your hopes for the future dashed. And today, some 70- or 80-plus years later you are still alive to talk about it. For many baby boomers that weren't alive yet during these depression years, they can still recite their parents' often said thoughts on going through these tough times. Thinking back, they can still hear the fear in their parents' voices. One minute they lived in a world where everything was basically the same: Father went to work in the morning and earned a paycheck to buy groceries and maybe a few of life's luxuries such as trips to the moving picture show, a major league baseball game, and, wonder of all wonders, a new motor car. Mother stayed at home and kept the home clean, made the meals and got the children through the day. Then one day, out of the blue, everything was turned upside down.

What Marketers Must Keep in Mind About the Great Depression

Because the fear of losing everything is still very real in the minds of many seniors, this is not a feeling to be taken lightly or glossed over by marketers. Elaine M. Doxie, in a piece for the website www.helium.com, reflects how many people who made it through the Great Depression never spent as freely as they did before that catastrophe occurred. The event, according to Ms. Doxie, ushered in an era of thrift. This was the result of one central belief: Another depression could be right around the corner and this time they were going to be prepared! For seniors who lived through this or saw this behavior in their parents, and baby boomers who saw similar characteristics in their parents or grandparents, it is something hard to get out of their minds, and may still be with them to this day, affecting their spending and buying habits.

Anne D'Innocenzio, a business writer for the Associated Press in a story "Consumers Change Buying Habits, But Will It Last" published in *USA Today* back on July 7, 2008, detailed how the most recent turbulent economic times have only brought out more examples of depression-era habits. She writes:

> *Some Americans say their parents or grandparents affected by the Great Depression are still hoarding buttons and squeezing out several soup meals from ham bones.*

Ms. D'Innocenzio's piece quotes then 88-year-old Edna Scott from Berkeley Heights, New Jersey, as saying:

> *I shop cautiously. I would say that is a hangover from the Great Depression.*

How must you shape your marketing message to crack this type of thinking from the likes of Ms. Scott, and those of her age range, let alone those in their 70s, 60s and down to their 50s, who have either been around such careful shoppers or heard stories of depression-era survivors who made several soup meals from ham bones?

Researcher Dr. Laura Portolese Dias, an author and professor at Shoreline Community College in Shoreline, Washington, studied buying habits of different generations in a report "Shopping Habits of Generation X'ers, Boomers and Matures: Buying Motivations of Our Generations." Her findings were published on the website www.prnewswire.com. Here she compared shopping patterns of those from Generation X (those born from the early to mid 1960s through the early 1980s) along with our two target groups (baby boomers and seniors, i.e. "matures"). One passage of note in Dr. Portolese Dias's report reads as follows:

> *People who experienced similar events together during formative childhood and teenage years tend to be similar in their buying habits. For example, the Great Depression or World War II generation lived through rationing on a daily basis for an extended period of time. Consequently, this generation demonstrates a more conservative and watchful spending when it comes to quantity and cost . . . they practice frugality as a way of life.*

This has very important implications, so let me reinforce its meaning: What it is saying is that you must, with seniors and some baby boomers, look to have them go against long-established beliefs and imbedded concerns that directly affect their buying habits.

This puts pressure on every aspect of your marketing. Seniors spend. But rarely thoughtlessly or casually. One of Dan Kennedy's constant cautions about marketing and selling applies perfectly here: Never underestimate the difficulty of the task!

As counterweight to the difficulty of getting senior consumers to override their conditioned frugality, they can be exceptionally valuable customers in terms of loyalty and referrals. While brand loyalty has been gradually losing a grip on boomers, it remains very influential with seniors, indicative of a predisposition to loyalty that can be leveraged by any marketer, with loyalty reward and incentive programs such as those provided by www.RoyaltyRewards.com—with customer newsletters and customer appreciation events, and other tactics touched on throughout this book—to increase the frequency of repeat patronage and block seduction by competing merchants or service providers. Also, extensive data mining in several different industries—from health care to travel—indicates that the senior customer's referral activity may naturally run as high as three times that of consumers in other age groups. All this has to be carefully considered in calculating total customer value and in making decisions about your willingness to "go the extra mile" as may be required to attract and sell to the senior in the first place.

In short, they may be the more reluctant spenders within the entire LEB/S market, yet there may be fewer businesses in your category directly and effectively competing for them, they may feel underserved or poorly served in your product or service category, and the value of their above-par loyalty and referrals may make them well worth special effort.

The point of this chapter is to emphasize that they are seniors and therefore have l-o-n-g histories, with life experiences and a frame of reference (see Chapter 10) that may be quite foreign to you, but can't be permitted to stay that way.

CHAPTER 5

In Many Ways, We Are Still Disappointingly Predictable

Dan Kennedy

I was once committed to retiring, independently wealthy, by age 44. Then by 55. Now by 60. I am, fortunately (but not luckily) independently wealthy, but I'm not retired. In this, I'm afraid I'm a cliché. The AARP Study (published in December, 2010), "Approaching 65: A Survey of Baby Boomers Turning 65 Years Old," reveals that most LEB/S pass through a succession of anticipated retirement dates.

In his book *Buy•ology: Truth and Lies About Why We Buy,* Martin Lindstrom refers to a study conducted by global advertising giant BBDO Worldwide, showing that in 26 different countries around the world, most of us perform exactly the same daily rituals. The first has been labeled by the study as "preparing for battle," when we rise in the morning and prepare to leave the privacy and security of our caves. A second they term "feasting"; eating with others—our penchant for the family breakfast, however hurried, or the gathering in the company break room to share the morning box of Dunkin' Donuts, the going to lunch together, the family dinner. Another, the final ritual of the day they call "protecting yourself from the future," is the rolling of the boulder into the cave door at night. For us, it's checking the doors, turning off the lights, maybe placing something with our car keys so we won't forget it in the morning. We are a very ritualistic and habit-driven people. Our religions influence us by engagement with ritual. Our communities control us by imposed ritual—you do have *a* trash day, don't you? There's *a* weekend when most of your community's residents haul out the outdoor Christmas decorations, right?

We are ritualistic buyers, too. LEB/S are more likely to grocery shop in an organized way, once a week, while younger people tend to hit-and-run shop, buying a few needed items, as often as four or five days during the week. But rituals exert much deeper influence than that. They exert influence over how we buy. The eagerness of sales professionals to close the sale at the first meeting is in conflict with most seniors and many LE-boomers' ritualistic way of making a buying decision, which is very often "sleeping on it," talking about it "over the weekend," and for those regular churchgoers with deep religious convictions, "praying over it." Fighting this by force is not as productive as catering to it and constructing a process for capitalizing on it. The LEB/S have high probability of a ritual for shopping for and ultimately buying an automobile, buying home furnishings, and many other goods and services, likely born of the rituals for such activities followed by their parents and their parents' peers. Further, they are likely to drift toward those rituals as they reach the age their parents were when engaging in them. If we know how a group's parents came to buy additional life insurance in their 50s, we know a lot about what will drive the group members to buy additional life insurance at age 50. The media used to get the message to them may have changed, but the message won't.

My friend, the seemingly near-psychic economist Harry Dent, Jr., has no psychic powers whatsoever. He is simply a great student of history, cycles, and most importantly, demographics and the movement of segments of the population from one demographic life stage to another. I urge studying Harry Dent, and refer you to his website: www.HSDent.com.

My colleague at GKIC, Dave Dee, creator of The Psychic Salesman System, a reformed magician and mentalist, has no actual psychic ability either, yet he can "foresee" what people will do and how they will react to different stimuli with near perfect accuracy. At the end of this chapter, you'll find a demonstration of human predictability from Dave, reprinted from GKIC's *No B.S. Marketing Letter,* which I edit. Years ago, I met and got to know a celebrated psychic named Richard Ireland, who regularly performed at the Playboy Clubs. He unerringly spotted and called out cheating spouses seated together in booths at his shows, ostensibly by reading their minds as he stalked the room. In reality, he was reading their body language as "not married," and noticing mismatched wedding rings. He told me he made his living by understanding the predictability of people. Richard's son, Mark, has recently republished his father's book *Your Psychic Potential* (www.MarkIrelandAuthor.com).

LEB/S folks are predictable. Despite massive societal, cultural, technological, and other changes that have occurred in the elapsed time between our fathers' passage through ages 50, 60, and beyond and our own, most of us will find more and more and more in common with our fathers at those ages. Clichés are us. As example, consider political leanings.

How Conservative Are LEB/S Consumers?

A Gallup poll conducted in early 2012 produced a fact shocking and disappointing to my clients in the financial services community, working with annuities, insurance, bonds and stocks, as well as to my clients in the real estate industry dealing with private investors: A full 40% of men and 28% of women overall, and about 60% of LEB/S men and 40% of LEB/S women rank *gold* as the best long-term investment. Not just safest. *Best*.

Keep in mind, gold yields no interest and pays no dividends. There is no cash flow. It is relatively illiquid. There is even precedent of risk of government confiscation—a historical artifact of that is reprinted on the next page in Figure 5.1. It's authentic. President Roosevelt did, in fact, demand that U.S. citizens turn their hoards of gold over to him. And most financial advisors, bankers, and accountants advise clients against buying it. With all that against it, still, 60% of LEB/S men rank it as the best investment. This speaks to a *very* conservative—and stubborn—mindset.

I mean no disrespect, but I often joke that if you visit the typical Glenn Beck listener's home, you may well find the cars parked outside because one half the garage is filled with gold bullion, the other half with dried survival food, seeds, guns, and ammo. But throughout the recession, the "gold bug" population has swelled, and the gold bullion, gold coin, and other hard-money advertisers haven't just populated the Glenn Beck and other ultraconservative radio talk show hosts' programming; they're all over the cable TV networks, in magazines, and in direct mail. Oh, and just for the record, if you stockpiled some gold when Mr. Beck began urging his listeners to do so, you have done well, and sacrificed negligible yield as other safe investments have paid near zero interest for almost five years at this writing. Although I'm not dispensing investment advice, I'm happy to report that I personally own gold

FIGURE 5.1: Gold Confiscation Exhibit

Executive Order 6102

UNDER EXECUTIVE ORDER OF THE PRESIDENT

issued April 5, 1933

all persons are required to deliver

ON OR BEFORE MAY 1, 1933

all **GOLD COIN, GOLD BULLION, AND GOLD CERTIFICATES** now owned by them to a Federal Reserve Bank, branch or agency, or to any member bank of the Federal Reserve System.

Executive Order

FORBIDDING THE HOARDING OF GOLD COIN, GOLD BULLION AND GOLD CERTIFICATES

FRANKLIN D. ROOSEVELT

THE WHITE HOUSE

For Further Information Consult Your Local Bank

GOLD CERTIFICATES may be identified by the words "GOLD CERTIFICATE" appearing thereon. The serial number and the Treasury seal on the face of a GOLD CERTIFICATE are printed in YELLOW. Be careful not to confuse GOLD CERTIFICATES with other issues which are redeemable in gold but which are not GOLD CERTIFICATES. Federal Reserve Notes and United States Notes are "redeemable in gold" but are not "GOLD CERTIFICATES" and are not required to be surrendered

Special attention is directed to the exceptions allowed under Section 2 of the Executive Order

CRIMINAL PENALTIES FOR VIOLATION OF EXECUTIVE ORDER
$10,000 fine or 10 years imprisonment, or both, as provided in Section 9 of the order

as part of my own diversified investment portfolio, and am damn glad I do. The point, though, is that the LEB/S consumer is generally more financially and politically/philosophically conservative than the rest of the population, and has moved further in those directions after the Wall Street crash, during the ensuing recession, and through the Obama administration. (Many gun dealers have had President Obama's photo framed and hung in their shops, labeled as "America's #1 Gun Salesman." The gold merchants undoubtedly have similar fond feelings.)

Consider this symbolic of the LEB/S attitude toward money. As Chip described in the previous chapter, seniors have intimate experience with the Great Depression and its chief lesson lingers: Everything can be wiped out overnight. Chip also pointed out that LE-boomers heard about that Great Depression, were lectured about its lessons endlessly, and programmed by parents to save for rainy days and worry over unseen dangers. While that advice may have been largely ignored when young, LE-boomers seem to return to it with age. Most of the financial advisors I've consulted with and coached find that the LEB/S clientele is much more concerned with safe preservation of capital than with gains or even yield.

LEB/S voters tend toward both fiscal and social conservatism too. Ronald Reagan is widely credited with observing that anyone who isn't liberal in youth has no heart but anyone who doesn't grow conservative with maturity has no brain. Actually, interestingly, ultra-affluent and wealthy LEB/S citizens often shift to ultra-liberal in their late years, but they are a carve-out from the rest; most LEB/S move farther and farther to the right of the political spectrum with age. This ties to marketing to them, because their attitudes about social, economic, and political issues offer opportunity for affinity and alignment.

A good demonstration of the LEB/S political conservatism can be found at the Media Research Center (MRC), where I've

"Good God! He's giving the white-collar voters' speech to the blue collars."

been a member of the Board of Trustees and have contributed political columns frequently to its www.BusinessAndMedia.org site. You'll find a complete look at the entire organization at www.MRC.org. The MRC operates as "America's Media Watchdog," monitoring virtually all broadcast and print, and a lot of online news media, for liberal bias, and churning out fact alerts, news releases, videos, sending its executives out to do interviews, and otherwise communicating to the media and the public in combat with liberal views. The MRC is completely supported by private donors, to the tune of over $10 million a year.

These are almost exclusively LEB/S donors, constantly in a state of dismay, disgust, and rage over the actions of politicians and liberal leanings of the press, and willing to pour money into an operation to be their voice and champion their views.

There is, in fact, no good reason to assume that the attitudinal and behavioral changes in people moving through their 50s, then 60s, and into their 70s will differ *substantially* from those who came before them. At the very least, historical precedents should be noted, understood, and considered by all marketers, with flexibility to new facts. If anything, the precise timing of the historical pattern will skew slower, later, older, as baby boomers fight their own aging of body and mind. But I am not in the camp with some age and age-wave experts who assert seismic change in LEB/S behavior. Sorry, but I don't see it. In fact, I think it's a fanciful and dangerous misread. I believe we are actually hard wired for attitudinal and behavioral change in relative concert with our passages through each 10-year segment of life. As an example, as the 60-year-old is more ready to shrink the size and scope of his life, his physical and health circumstances are asking him to do so. And more so at 65. And more so at 70. Obviously, different people do age differently. We all know people in their 50s acting 70, and in their 70s acting 50. Joan Rivers is a past client of mine; I admire her and I have a friendly relationship with her, and she has absolutely defied age. In the harness races I drive in professionally, the majority of the drivers I compete against are 20 years my junior or even younger, but there are several good drivers pushing 70, one, 75. Such people who contradict age by their activities often violate age's common trajectory of attitude change. But these people represent a relative minority, and while inspirational to the rest, are not all that influential with the rest's actual thinking and behavior. If you are to wager with odds in your favor as a marketer, you will pay close attention to historical precedents.

The Del Webb 2010 survey of all boomers suggests that the conservative lean won't be changing anytime soon. The Woodstock group reveals the greatest tendency to have become more conservative with age. Boomers who turned 50 in 2010 shifted 26% more conservative, those who turned 50 in 1996 have shifted 45% more conservative. Only 18% and 13%, respectively, cite shifting to more liberal views. Seniors and LE-boomers both named Ronald Reagan on their lists of top three heroes.

The Trick: E-Z Mindreading

(Just follow along and you'll experience the trick!)

- Pick A Number Between 1 and 10
- Multiply It By 9
- Add the Digits Together
- Subtract 5
- Identify the Alphabet Letter That Corresponds With Your Number
- Quickly Think of a Country That Begins with That Letter
- Using That Country's Second Letter, Instantly Think of an Animal Beginning With That Letter
- Now Think Of That Animal's Color

Turn to the next page and see what I predicted you would think of.

Secret: The combination of psychology and math make this trick work nearly 100% of the time as long as you follow the script!

The Trick: E-Z Mindreading

You're thinking of a gray elephant in Denmark!

Dave Dee Demonstration, Excerpted from the *No B.S. Marketing Letter,* June 2012

CHAPTER 6

Mars and Venus

Dan Kennedy

LEB/S women and LEB/S men are different. Duh.

Their motivations are different. Some years back, I worked on the creative team writing and producing a TV infomercial for a pain relief product—one of the first, in what is now becoming a fairly crowded category. We were ahead of the LEB / S Age-Profit Wave and only generated a few million dollars. Today, that same show for that same product would likely do $50 million, direct-response plus retail combined. Anyway, I wound up spending a full day talking with people in their early 60s into their 70s about their arthritis. It became crystal clear that arthritis meant something very different to women than to men.

For women, arthritis meant three things. First, interference with their ability to do things they enjoyed, like gardening,

knitting, wrapping gifts elegantly, and cooking. Two, harm to their role in their family. Of particular angst, now *needing* daughter or (worse) daughter-in-law assistance in the kitchen when cooking a big family dinner. Three, poor appearance, like gnarled hands. One compared her hands to "the gnarled old oak tree in the backyard."

For men, arthritis meant one very big thing: needing someone's help, typically the wife's help, in doing ordinary man things like buttoning a shirt, using cufflinks, tying neckties, or being relieved of or embarrassed in front of others—even just his wife—by being unable to perform basic man duties, like twisting open a stubborn jar lid. It wasn't the not being able to do 'x' that sparked angst or rage. It was needing help. Being seen as impaired.

For both, needing help was an emotional trigger. But for her, it was more that inability to do things. For him, it was totally about needing help. My guess is that these meanings of arthritis may not hold the same power over people now 40 or 30 when they reach 50, 60, and 70, but the current seniors are totally anchored to traditional 1950 male/female, husband/wife roles and duties, and today's LE-boomers are still significantly anchored to the same images and self-images.

Their responses to their relationships are different. A trek to the largest physical bookstore you can find, then title-by-title examination of all the books in the sociology, psychology, and self-help aisles is extremely educational, about men and women of all ages, and of LEB/S men and women. There are lots of books for women about relationships with daughters, with sisters, with parents, co-workers, and husbands. There are only a few for men about their relationships with sons, brothers, parents, co-workers and wives. There is growth in three LEB/S categories: one, what to do with a retired man on your hands; two, how to cope with adult children who have moved back in; three, how to handle new caregiver responsibilities. These books are all aimed at women. If men buy self-help books, they are about how to fix things such as cars and houses; how to win at things such as golf and poker; and how to invest in things, such as stocks and real estate. They aren't about relationships. The LEB/S woman is coping with a myriad of personal emotional issues, is leaning into spiritual questions and thinking, is handling empty-nest or boomerang-back-into-nest issues, dealing with new dynamics in the marital relationship, shouldering the elderly parent problems, and more. She looks for information, inspiration, consolation, and support for all these things on the bookshelves, in magazines, online, with friends, at church, and from businesses, products, and services from providers "who understand." The LEB/S man is also facing many issues, but for the most part, he prefers solving them with silence, a blue pill, or a hammer.

Their responses to appearance remain very different. Very few men buy anti-wrinkle creams. Women buy virtually endless amounts, trying one new one after another after another after another, and the age of these buyers is expanding down and up, from a fairly tight 50 to 60 just a half-decade ago, to 35 to 75 now. Women obsess over their hair and buy endless varieties of hair care glop, too. Rogaine has been a tough sell to men. Most pay little attention to what shampoo they buy (or is bought for them), and the overwhelming majority going bald settle with it. I recently advised a company doing radio commercials for two LEB/S products: a "miracle" shampoo for women, and a herbal alternative to Viagra® for men. The first drafts of the spots were product-focused. For the shampoo, I recommended adding in that her friends would be asking her what she had done with her hair, and that—miracle of miracles—even the man in her life would notice (a rarely fulfilled but persistent hope of women every time they return from the salon). For the magic pill, I recommended adding that he would be free of anxiety, stop avoiding sex and never disappoint and be embarrassed by disappointing the woman in his life again. I tweaked the spots to be LEB/S centric rather than product/features and benefits centric.

Their reactions to their adult kids tend to differ. As Chip laid out in Chapter 3, a huge shift has taken place from the adult kids killing to be free and independent, and very often providing financial and other support to their parents, to being dependents of their parents well into their 20s and 30s. Mothers tend to be concerned, worried, and tolerant. Fathers tend to be disappointed.

LEB/S women are very cause-driven and supportive. For many social responsibility charities, such as environment, animal rescue, medical/search for the cure, and food banks, LEB/S women outnumber LEB/S men as donors by a 3–1 to 5–1 margin (which should tell them all who to focus on and how to craft their messages). LEB/S men tend to outnumber LEB/S women by 2–1 to 3–1 as donors to political organizations, causes, and campaigns. LEB/S women consumers are far more influenced by a business's affiliation with and support of social causes and charities than are men. Some companies go "all in" on this, like the Stonyfield Farms organic foods company's sponsorships of its own Stonyfield Farms Strong Women's summits, retreats, and books that have sold millions of copies, and social network of "women supporting women in living healthier lives." When you visit the www.stonyfield.com website, or visit its Facebook site, you are invited into a vibrant online community. They were well into this in the mid-2000s. Many companies are following suit. The financial advisory community that I've been doing a lot of consulting with in recent years includes a number of female, seven-figure income advisors either entirely specializing in marketing to and providing services to women, or at least operating a branded business of that kind alongside their open-to-all LEB/S practice, and they all connect themselves to women's issues and causes and to social charities.

Last, LEB/S women worry more about money than LEB/S men do, arguably marking them as more sensible about money than men. Data drawn from "The Impact of Retirement Risk on Women," conducted by the Society of Actuaries in 2011, shows differences in many money matters:

- Being able to preserve the value of savings and investments: 55% of men cite it as a concern, 60% of women. Wider spreads occur in more specific scenarios…
- Not being able to maintain same standard of living for life: 39% of men list as chief worry, 50% of women.
- Not being able to stay in current home: 26% men, 38% women.
- Having finances destroyed by ill health: 39% men, 55% women.
- Not being able to leave desired amounts of money to children and grandchildren: not as big a deal as the financial services industry thinks, and basically an even split: 27% men, 28% women.

In virtually every area of thought, emotion, behavior, and buying behavior, they're different. LEB/S male buyers are far more facts, functionality, and results-oriented. LEB/S female buyers are far more trust, sense of security, and relationship-oriented. In the book by Mary Brown and Carol Orsborn Ph.D., *BOOM: Marketing to the Ultimate Power Consumer, the Baby Boomer Woman*, key appeals to the women are summarized this way:

1. For the conventional LEB/S: Tell her you can give her the help she needs and that you will keep her safe.

2. For the transitional to LE-boomer woman: Tell her that you believe in her.
3. For the aspirational, younger boomer woman: Tell her that you will embrace life with her.

This ties products/services and their providers to safety and security and done-for-you, to recognition of life experience, capability, wisdom, or to inspiration, motivation, vision, and ambition—depending on where the boomer woman is in age and mindset.

I would peg the same age groupings of males *somewhat* differently. For the first group, appeal to preservation of self-determination, self-reliance, independence, and authority, with a quiet, very private concern for safety and security. For the second, give them the same sort of recognition but coupled with a very explicit promise of the male consumer being in charge; being king of his castle; being entirely trustworthy and capable of making the necessary decisions. In this same vein, market to their sense of choosing to use certain products for convenience's sake or as "better life boosters," but not out of need born of diminished capacity. At the time I'm writing this, the effective TV ads for Viagra® state that, "This is the age of getting things done and you don't let anything stand in your way." For the third group of boomer men, the "we'll embrace life together" idea is applicable, but the language is not. The word "embrace" is a profoundly female LEB/S word.

Your need to master the marketing that works with LEB/S women is simple: The LEB/S women control the money. In fact, the males become less significant and influential in consumer spending as they age; the females ever more in control. Two-thirds of the consumer wealth is under the control of women, and LEB/S women make up the largest demographic of this purchasing gender, making or strongly influencing as much as 80% of the buying decision—and in certain categories, like health care, virtually controlling 100% of the action (source: MetLife Mature Market Research). The number of LEB/S women remaining in the workforce past age 55, and again past age 65, is significantly greater than men, and the spread is growing, and projected to grow. Not only are they continuing to earn income, they are disproportionately benefiting from wealth transfer by inheritance from grandparents, parents, and husbands.

Even in categories often thought of as male territory, industry research in each reveals women in control of 80% of home improvement decisions, 50% of consumer electronics purchases, and 65% of new auto purchases.

The fast-growing segment of new, small-business startups is boomer women, and over half of all small businesses registered with a male owner are actually husband-wife managed, often with the woman in charge of the money.

"Gotta run, sweetheart. By the way, that was one fabulous job you did raising the children."

Outright segregation can be tricky. Boomer women respond very badly to any sense that they are being sent out of the room or seated at the little people's table. At GKIC, we wrestle this alligator with the annual conferences for women entrepreneurs, relatively new in the company's portfolio of events, and intended to spawn segregated coaching programs, products, and services. However, boomer and LEB/S women *do* want what is *for them,* and there is powerful advantage in providing it, despite the difficulty in some product or business categories.

The delivery of different marketing messages to the different LEB/S genders is essential for optimum results.

CHAPTER 7

The Exceptionally Affluent LEB/S

Dan Kennedy

High levels of affluence and net worth are exceptional, but not all that exceptional among LEB/S. They have, after all, had time to accumulate savings. They have been programmed more to save rather than spend than trailing-edge boomers and younger groups. An inordinate percentage have started and built their own businesses and companies, the most reliable path to wealth. Many others have benefited from following a progressive career path of 20, 30, even 40 years with the same employer and there accumulating significant pension benefits—that "40 Year Plan" all but gone from society for today's young people. But given all these factors, you will still likely be surprised by the average net worth of today's LEB/S retirees: *$708,000.00*, based on U.S.

government data and a "Mature Market Research Study" by Cogent Research, conducted in 2010–2011. A full one-third of affluent LE-boomers has fully retired and is included in the group with this $708,000.00 average net worth.

While this is a very respectable number, it is still insufficient to guarantee a level lifestyle over remaining years, let alone insulate against the uncertainties of rising health-care costs or a catastrophic health event or re-emergence of significant inflation, particularly given the low to near-zero yield of the safest fixed-income investments continuing as this book is being written. Even a 5% yield on $700,000.00 fully invested only produces $35,000.00, less capital gains taxes, but 1% produces a miserly $7,000.00. A great many retired LEB/S have been eating principal for recent years' living expenses. Further, that $708,000.00 nest egg is down 12% from its peak in 2007–2008. Since retirees cannot replace nest egg losses with active earnings, even these affluent LEB/S are anxious about money.

The biggest change in reality and sense of stability that retirement brings to anybody is the absence of regular weekly or monthly paychecks. The Mutual Fund Store directly addresses this with its radio commercials talking about their plan to create regular retirement *paychecks*. The use of that specific word—paycheck—is definitely not accidental. The end of active earning is a big psychological Rubicon. Earlier in this book, Chip wrote about the "new numbers" of people postponing retirement and the many reasons for their doing so, not all of which are financial. As someone who could have quit working to earn money about five years ago, with my net worth target achieved, and by my calculations (as an eat-the-principal, "die broke" guy) more than enough money to outlast my terrestrial body, I have found myself very reluctant to turn off the earnings tap. Part of this is, I suppose, tied to having witnessed my parents at essentially zero net worth in their later years, and entirely dependent on me plus the government for basic necessities, an emotional and psychological imprint comparable to the Great Depression experience of seniors that Chip described in Chapter 4. I've had conversations about this "Why are we still working? And working so hard?" thing with quite a few other very affluent LEB/S people who are my clients or peers. Most, like me, are entrepreneurs or in high-profile careers, so there is compulsion, self-concept linkage to work (we are what we do), an absence of outside interests, disinclination to socialize with "civilians," and other ingrained behavioral factors in play, which we privately acknowledge as our own psychosis. But most also have some significant frame of reference, either from the formative years or from a financial crash-and-burn on their zigzag path to success, that cautions against stopping the making of money. Many give lip service to impending retirement, but that doesn't mean you can seem to push it or accept it as authentic motivation when marketing and selling to them—make a note of that.

It's also important to keep firmly in mind how very high the desire for lifetime self-sufficiency is with the successful and affluent LEB/S. In the 1940s, 1950s, and into the 1960s, the secular religion of America was self-reliance. Dependence on others in any shape or form, including government subsidy, was shameful. Today, we've moved to the polar opposite: a new ideology of entitlement and shame-free, guilt-free acceptance of all manner of government hand-outs, from college students demanding "free" contraceptives, to the extension of unemployment benefits to 99 weeks, to mortgage principal write-downs, to you-name-it. JFK's famous line including the phrase, "Ask not what your country can do for you" will land on deaf ears today with most younger than LEB/S, as well as some in LEB/S. But LEB/S "came up" and made their way devoutly believing in self-reliance, and those who created from-scratch wealth are most deeply committed to that ideal. *Their mindset is to never be in need.*

In marketing to them, despite their affluence and the ease of affording whatever you sell that exists, you can never be casual about asking them to spend money.

I was once at a meeting at the home of a retired Fortune 500 company's CEO, something of an iconic figure whose name you would almost certainly know. When we interrupted our work to go out and grab a quick lunch, he led the way through the line at a nearby fast-food joint and, reaching the cashier, produced a coupon. Later, when the others had left his home, I asked him about it. I would estimate his net worth in the $50 million to $100 million range, and in his late 70s at the time, thus extremely unlikely to outlive his fortune, so capturing a few dollars of savings with a coupon seemed odd enough to question. Rather sheepishly, he said his housekeeper knew he liked this particular restaurant and insisted on clipping its coupons from her Sunday newspaper and placing them on the desk in his study, and, since they were money just the same as the green money printed by the government, he felt guilty throwing them out. "After all," he said, "what would my mother think of that?"

SECTION 2

STRATEGIES

CHAPTER 8

The Power of Profiling

Dan Kennedy

In this book, Chip and I have been making some sweeping generalizations about LEB/S consumers. These are necessary because this is a book intended for broad diversity of business owners, entrepreneurs, and professionals. But you have an avatar client, an ideal customer, a very particular person within LEB/S who lives in your particular community or operates in your industry. He is an individual, not a human envelope filled with statistics. The more clarity you get about your customer, the better you can serve him, the more successfully and affordably you can attract and acquire him.

There are many different ways to subdivide any market. There are niches and subculture. A niche is occupational or vocational. Auto mechanics are in an occupational niche, as are auto repair shop owners, however, the owners and mechanics think very differently about many things, probably pay different prices for shirts, dine at different kinds of restaurants, and so on, and are likely to carry those differences all the way into retirement. A subculture has to do with interests, shared experiences, and backgrounds. College alumni: subculture. Tea Party: subculture. Harley-Davidson owners: subculture. (Side note: LEB/S are the top Harley-Davidson buyers.) There are demographics: Age. Gender. Marital status. Life cycles, and life-passages positions, such as LE-boomer, trailing-edge boomer, and senior. Income and wealth differential.

Geography can be over-rated and under-rated. Geo-demographic profiling is based on the idea that you are where you live, from the old tenet that birds of a feather flock together. Companies now spend large sums having their customer files run through geo-demo analytics, dividing them into 50 to 65 different "clusters" and about a dozen "social groups." Different analytics companies use different terminology for the groups, such as Suburban Status Seekers and Affluent Traditionalists. This is pitched as a "simple way to identify, understand, and target consumers." It is simple, but it is also severely flawed, and, by and large, I am not a fan. For certain kinds of fairly large consumer marketers it has a place, and it can provide data that, if used in concert with other data, is helpful. It can at least be used to rule out lowest probability clusters for direct mail. It can be used to tweak copy, broadly. But it is cutting-edge science hooked to a very antiquated idea: that we cluster together by physical neighborhoods. This is just not so. While I am rather reclusive, I know a few things about my own immediate neighbors. Our homes all cost about the same and look about the same, but mine houses a large home office and meeting space in its basement; a neighbor's houses a pool table and poker room. Most here are LE-boomers, a couple are seniors, a couple are younger, one is in a minority group, all others are white. My income is at least five times any of the neighbors' and I know it to be a full ten times at least one of them. I am the only one who owns classic cars. Or racehorses. Only one owns a boat. One is a constant world traveler. I abhor international travel. Need I go on?

Today, the birds flock together on social media more so than by neighborhoods. Sure, parents with young children tend to cluster around schools. That sort of thing is obvious. But again, generalizing about all the parents in a radius around a school is less viable than it was a decade ago. Diversity has invaded a great many neighborhoods in many ways.

There is an excellent, more in-depth discussion of segmentation in the book *Marketing to the Mindset of Boomers and Their Elders* by Carol Morgan. We are in agreement in skepticism about simplified marketing by geo-demo clusters. We also share agreement on another key point: A segmentation strategy should be based on multiple, redundant measures. In other words, more than one source of information overlapped with another is best. I'm not often looking for simple. I'm looking for most effective.

Data mining as well as psychographic mining of your own customers—and of only your best clients you'd most like to clone—is always a good start. Maybe they do cluster geographically. Maybe they are within a tight age range within the LEB/S market. Maybe they all golf. Data may be in your records. The fact that they all golf or attend the theater or vacation in Florida may only be found by asking, by surveying, by gathering information.

Ultimately, you should build a profile of your customer target.

One of the very best examples of this kind of profiling, that shocks many when I show it to them because it strikes them as predatory, is from the famous pastor Rick Warren. You should recognize him as the author of the mega-best-selling book, *The Purpose-Driven Life.* He is the founder of the huge Saddleback

Church. You should obtain and study his not-so-famous book, *The Purpose-Driven Church.* It is a marketing manual for pastors. In it he describes in stark and specific detail the profile of "Saddleback Sam," their ideal parishioner, who they deliberately target—ignoring and excluding a lot of other people. He teaches each pastor to create such a profile.

Carol Morgan advances some lifestyle/life-passages-based profiles for LEB/S. I'll just list them and describe them as briefly as possible, as thought-starters for how you might categorize your customers/target customers:

- *Upbeat Enjoyers*. Optimistic, active, involved. Interested in looking, feeling, and acting younger than their years. Consider retirement a continuation of life, not a destination point marked by a stop sign.
- *Insecures*. Pessimistic, deeply troubled by their lack of financial success and/or by ill health. They view society as obsessed with youth and beauty, and discriminatory and unjust toward them.
- *Threatened Actives*. Concerned with preserving their independence, remaining in their own homes, continuing to drive their own cars. Have a rather traditional attitude toward retirement and a resigned acceptance of aging.
- *Financial Positives*. Responsible, organized planners, conservatively invested, trying not to work in retirement. Most receptive to relocating and possibly moving into a retirement community.

As you can see, these are incomplete profiles. You can also see they might now live in the same zip code or even on the same street, they might even have had similar starting points in life, and other similarities, but it's their profound differences that matter. If you are going to resonate with them, you must speak to each one very differently. Or if you want one as your customer, you must be willing to repel the others and design everything you say and do to match the one desired. In her book, Morgan builds profiles like these, but specific to different product/service segments, such as travel, in which there are Highway Wanderers but also Pampered Relaxers and Global Explorers.

Resource

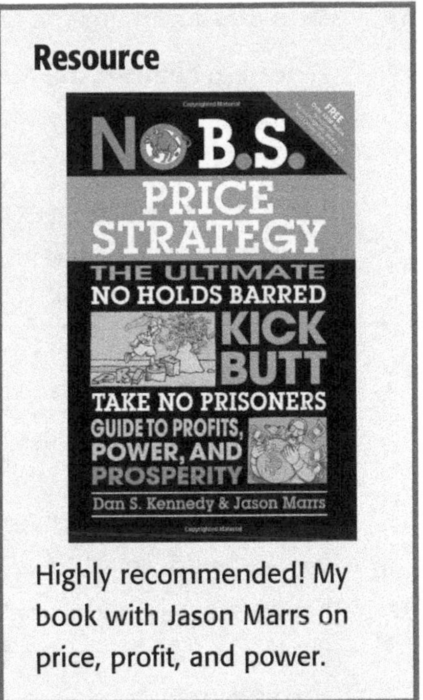

Highly recommended! My book with Jason Marrs on price, profit, and power.

Because I am a price strategy guy, I would think in terms of different consumers' thinking about price. There are, for example, Committed Coupon Clippers, who will always buy by price and will choose brands, pick restaurants, etc., based on price or on actually having a coupon in hand. There are Value Buyers, who are concerned with price, but not in a vacuum. There are Complex Buyers, who place many other factors ahead of price, such as expertise, service, and convenience. There are Status Buyers and Elitists. Etc. Most people move about a bit from one of these groups to another, depending on what they are buying.

Again, the more clarity and specificity you can get to with your profile of your desired LEB/S consumer, the better.

There are four chief ways to use your profile:

1. As basis for "attraction copy" in lead-generation advertising
2. In "elevator speech" prospecting, in person-to-person selling
3. In selecting and renting commercially available mailing lists and segments thereof

4. In message matching to segments.

In lead-generation advertising, we often focus on the person we want to attract, rather than the product or service being sold. The simplest template for these is the profile. For example:

> TAX AND FINANCIAL ALERT FOR THE 55- TO 65-YEAR-OLD SMALL-BUSINESS OWNER CONCERNED WITH RETIREMENT OR FAMILY SUCCESSION ISSUES. If you own a small business worth at least $500,000.00 to $5 million, are getting serious about retirement, married with children or adult children, and unsure of the best strategic options for structuring safe, guaranteed income for life, the author of the best-selling book, *Navigation Guide to Rich Retirement and Executive Director of the Southwest Asset Preservation Center*, William K. Stewart, has new, timely, and important information you need before making any decisions. See his 20-minute video presentation at EndOfIncome.com or call (000) 000-0000 to receive a free DVD sent by mail, no obligation, no salesperson involved. There may be a TAX TIME BOMB HIDING INSIDE YOUR SUCCESSFUL BUSINESS! Find out at www.EndofIncome.com.

As you can see, virtually nothing about the products or services offered is said. The ad is a construct of profile plus offer, little more. And it could even be further abbreviated to strip out the advertiser's identity:

> TAX AND FINANCIAL ALERT FOR THE 55- TO 65-YEAR-OLD SMALL-BUSINESS OWNER CONCERNED WITH RETIREMENT OR FAMILY SUCCESSION ISSUES. If you own a small business worth at least $500,000.00 to $5 million, are getting serious about retirement, married with children or adult children, and unsure of the best strategic options for structuring safe, guar-

> anteed income for life, you should see the new, timely, and important 20-minute video presentation at EndOfIncome.com, or call (000) 000-0000 to receive a free DVD sent by mail, no obligation, no salesperson involved. There may be a TAX TIME BOMB HIDING INSIDE YOUR SUCCESSFUL BUSINESS! Find out at www.EndofIncome.com.

With the "elevator speech," the answer to "What do you do?" for cocktail party conversation, a very similar approach is used, placing the emphasis on the profile rather than the product or service, or instantly, easily dismissed description of your business or profession. Stick with this example, the answer would begin:

> I work with 55- to 65-year-old small-business owners concerned with retirement or family succession issues, who own a business worth at least $500,000.00 to $5 million, are getting serious about retirement, are married with children or adult children, and unsure of the best strategic options for structuring safe, guaranteed income for life . . .

In renting commercially available mailing lists, the profile is essential to the search. The starting point for this, incidentally, is at www.SRDS.com. You can also learn a great deal from the list search and selection expert I and my clients work with, Craig Simpson, at www.simpson-direct.com.

Finally, the profile allows you to alter and match your basic message to different segments of lists. For example, here are slightly different blocks of copy from the outer envelopes, sent to different age segments of the same business owner and business magazine subscriber lists, for a product and membership offer for GKIC (similar to the gift offer for you shown on page 264):

1. You worked hard to build your business and your life. Every success, earned. Don't you just wonder about the generation behind you and the world we live in? It seems upside down: achievement punished, irresponsibility rewarded. Being an entrepreneur can make you feel like the odd man out . . .
2. You are working very hard to build your business—even sacrificing time with your family to do it. You have ideas, ambition, drive, determination . . .
3. Your friends, neighbors, most people your age are totally into their kids, family and entertainment, and recreation. To them, you're strange. You have ideas, ambition, drive. You're willing to invest endless hours in building your business . . .

You should be able to identify which paragraph is aimed at which age group: LEB/S, trailing-edge boomers, and the next age group behind the trailing-edge boomers. They were actually matched paragraph 1 to ages 55 to 65, paragraph 2 to 35 to 55, and paragraph 3 to 25 to 35. You should also be able to see how this demographic customization of the message matters and can lift the response rate.

Most marketers, particularly small-business level marketers, are not nearly this sophisticated. They cast overly broad, generic marketing messages to everybody within their target zip codes, at one website to which all traffic is routed, even to their own customers for whom they should have segmentation data. If you will make yourself more sophisticated, you'll gain competitive advantage and likely boost the profitability of your business as well.

The Power of Reality

There is academic theory, then there is reality.

Michael Lynn, a professor of the Cornell School of Hotel Administration, told *Nation's Restaurant News* that, "The old strategy of segmenting a marketplace and then appealing to different demographics—I don't buy it. Fundamentally, consumers don't differ that much from one another."

Professor Lynn is making a dangerously foolish statement.

First of all, demographic market or list segmentation is not an "old" strategy. In fact, in the direct-marketing world, the old power players were guys like me—the idea people, the copywriters. The new power players are the data mining wizards. My friend, the celebrated economist Harry Dent, Jr., has been more on-target than most with financial and societal predictions precisely because he focuses so heavily on the influence of demographics, and I strongly recommend reading Dent (www.HSDent.com).

Second, I can assure you, from millions of dollars of real-world marketing experience in place of academic theory, that nothing lifts response better than slicing and segmenting markets, lists, or audiences by demographics and by psychographics, and speaking to them differently. Contrary to the prof's assertion, I'll tell you that consumers differ enormously from one another. My friends involved in political campaigns and fundraising would laugh at the professor. They know that the population of northeast Ohio is profoundly different in an important array of attitudes and behaviors from the population of southern Ohio, and that East Clevelanders differ significantly from West Siders, that ethnicity matters, that

The Power of Reality

religious and political affiliations matter. Some media like TV tends to force generic, or "big net" messages, but a great deal of political marketing is about precision, with very different messages directed even to different mailboxes on the same street.

Nothing is more powerful in marketing than *customization*, and I'd say that is treble true with LEB/S (see Chapter 17). Demographics are an essential tool for customization.

CHAPTER 9

Advantages in Marketing to LEB/S

Dan Kennedy

There are excellent reasons for preferring LEB/S as your target market, in addition to the fact that roughly half of all the money is in these hands. These are advantages you want to take full advantage of:

1. Classic credibility matters.
2. They accept advice from authority.
3. They prefer mail, open mail, read mail.
4. They will read lengthy material.
5. They value books, articles, and news media.
6. They will listen to/watch lengthy presentations.
7. They act responsibly, so they can be obligated.
8. They are courteous and generally can be trained to be good customers.

9. They are charitable
10. They can be good centers of influence and sources of referrals

Classic Credibility at Work

The younger the consumer, the less concern with classic credibility exists. If they're under 30, they have grown up online. Doing business with a bank formed yesterday, with no brick-and-mortar offices, is perfectly normal to them. A bank that was founded in 1913, survived the Great Depression, never defaulted to a single depositor, and has had offices in the community for 40 years has no advantage with them. Longevity is not persuasive, and may even be viewed as a detriment. This is the exact opposite mindset to that of the LEB/S. For those born from 1946 through the 1950s, "Our 25th year of service to the families of Oakbrook" means something. For older seniors, it means everything.

While I was writing this, my wife and I were discussing the ten-year warranty being offered by a particular company. She said, "That's IF they're around to honor it." That would not so quickly occur to our 40-year-old daughter, and it probably wouldn't occur to a 30-year-old at all.

To the LEB/S consumer, longevity can be translated into credibility, which can be translated into security and safety, a chief driver for seniors, and a significant driver for LE-boomers.

The same is true about other security statistics, like numbers of clients served, years clients have stayed, the size of a company. To the LEB/S, the ultimate credibility is what I call "Leadership Position." When you can define your company as THE leader in a category (even if you have to cleverly create the category), you have valuable credibility, thus security and safety to sell. My wife's skepticism about the ten-year warranty can be allayed with facts about that manufacturer's longevity and leadership position in its field—with her. But those same facts would be unpersuasive to much younger consumers. My client, the Guthy-Renker Corporation, owns this oddity with its famous acne treatment product, Proactiv®. It actually has the leadership position, as the #1 best-selling acne treatment, with great longevity, and connection to prominent dermatologists. These facts are meaningful to the parents of the teen and preteen users, although not nearly as useful as they would be if selling to the grandparents. But the same facts are utterly uninteresting to the teens and preteens. They only want to know if it works, how easy it is to use and how fast it works. Their attention can be gained with endorsements from celebrities like Justin Bieber. But they have no patience for discussions of leadership position credibility.

Since this kind of credibility is persuasive to the LEB/S consumer, you want to make full use of whatever of it you have. If you have longevity, if you have leading citizens or institutions as customers, if yours is a third-generation family business, if you have leadership position, by all means trumpet it, and try not to omit it from any delivery of your advertising or sales message.

Because I Said So

LEB/S consumers were raised under the Because I Said So doctrine, and a good many parented, taught, and coached under the same doctrine. They are conditioned and accustomed to accept authority. Seniors, for example, are still significantly interested by political endorsements from their city's newspaper editors, civic groups, business groups, and their own political party's leaders, while, as you drop in age, these endorsements seem to be of no value to candidates whatsoever. Seniors are also the most supportive of the traditional doctrine of their particular church or religion. Seniors and a good percentage of LE-boomers tend to "do what the doctor tells them."

This conditioned behavior is useful to the advertiser, marketer, or sales professional who can establish authority and gain acceptance as an authority figure with LEB/S prospects and clientele. In my work with clients in various fields selling to LEB/S clients or patients, with a two-appointment selling process (diagnostic, then prescriptive) I have proven without exception that the acceptance of treatment or financial plan at that second appointment can be substantially improved by bestowing the trappings of authority on the advisor or doctor. These professionals' conversion percentages go up, and case sizes go up, and fee resistance goes down when we make them authors of books, guest experts seen on local or, better, national TV programs, and heard interviewed on local or, better, national radio programs, published in newspapers and financial magazines, placed on university or charity advisory boards, properly displaying these things in their offices, and sending prospects such material before and between appointments. In short, when the salesman ceases being the salesman and becomes the exalted authority, just like the doctor, his prescription is accepted without quarrel.

They Have Good Attention Span

Attention span matters, and the LEB/S consumer has more of it than any other consumers, so they will read long letters and articles, read books, watch full-length presentations, and listen to long audio recordings during a sales process. This book does not afford the time and space to make the lengthy, thoroughly documented and decisive case for length in ad copy, in sales letters and other media, and in sales presentations. I make it elsewhere, and I'll ask the skeptics to investigate elsewhere. I will only take a few minutes to appeal to logic, common sense, and what you can see with your own eyes. Common sense tells you that forced abbreviation of a presentation, however it is delivered, can make the task of persuasion more difficult. Logic should tell you that intellectual interest and emotional commitment grow given time, and the more time somebody invests in learning about something or someone, the more likely they are to go forward with a purchase or relationship. These are the reasons for enormously successful staples in direct marketing, like the *30-minute* TV infomercial (even if about a seemingly simple product, like a countertop grill), the *16- to 64-page* "magalogs" used by alternative health and financial newsletter publishers and by nutritional supplement companies—mailed in the tens of millions every year—catalogs that consume *20 to 30 minutes* to page through, the *two- to three-hour* open-to-public seminars and workshops used by financial advisors, implant dentists, and other professionals to interest LEB/S consumers in their services.

In my own experience, for making money nothing trumps a well-written 16- to 64-page sales letter delivered by the postman. Provided it is going to somebody who is prone to open and read it, and that *is* the LEB/S consumer.

In many cases, such letters are accompanied by additional literature, a DVD that may be 30 to 60 minutes in length, and an audio CD that may be equally long or longer. **My objective is usually to get a prospect to spend at least 30 minutes learning about my or my client's proposition, while seated comfortably in his favorite recliner, on the couch, at the kitchen table. My goal is never brevity.** Because this is the most effective approach to marketing and selling, it is a huge benefit to be selling to LEB/S consumers who will cooperate and participate in it. Don't waste that advantage!

The LEB/S also has a healthy respect for media. The senior's home is more likely to have a library filled with books, *hardcover* books, than a media room. Noted elsewhere, the LEB/S still reads and respects the newspaper. The network evening news programs are hanging on, almost entirely viewed by LEB/S. This is an advantage you can capitalize on by authoring a book or books of your own, by getting into print in the newspaper and magazines and utilizing the reprints, by advertising on news programs on TV and radio. To be clear, the new media that is accepted as substitute by younger consumers does not serve the same purpose for you with LEB/S consumers. Your own internet radio show is not the same as your own real radio show or even being interviewed on real radio programs. Your own YouTube video is not the same as real TV. Your blog is not the same as a column in the real newspaper. Jon Stewart, the host of *The Daily Show*, the Comedy Channel's news-satire program very popular with viewers much younger than LEB/S, revealed something about his own age and mindset when, after being hectored by Arianna Huffington about repeatedly refusing to write a blog on her site, exasperatedly said, "Why would I do *that?* I have *real* media. I have a *real* TV show."

Subject to "Good Guilt"

Seniors are mostly very civilized, responsible, do-the-right-thing folks. They try to be good neighbors. They tend to return favors. In the nonprofit fundraising world, one of the most frequently used direct-mail gimmicks is the enclosure of a gift (in marketing lingo, a freemium), often preprinted return address labels, with a fundraising solicitation. This is done most often and works best with mail aimed at seniors. Why? Because they'll want to keep the labels, they'll even feel guilty throwing them out—*after all, they're useful; waste not, want not; and somebody went to all the trouble to make them for me.* But they'll also feel guilty keeping them but throwing out the sender's letter unread. It's rude. So they'll play fair and read the letter, and they start out a little predisposed to donating if given a convincing argument. I call this "good guilt." It can help get done what I want people to do, and that's a good thing!

The reigning authority on the psychology of this, sometimes called the theory of reciprocity, is Dr. Robert Cialdini, a professor at Arizona State University, corporate consultant, and author of the mega-best-selling book, *Psychology of Influence.* He and I have been on several programs together as speakers, exchanged information, and I've brought him in to work with one of my coaching/mastermind groups. I urge getting and reading his book, or to start, visiting his website at www.influenceatwork.com. Everything he describes about the theory of reciprocity applies to the senior market, and will work best there.

LE-boomers are also very subject to motivation by guilt, but in other ways. They tend to be hypersensitive to failing at being "super-parents." Many even start second families with new spouses relatively late in life, in order to "get it right the second time." This can be a leveragable emotion when selling to them if they are still parents with young children, or if you are selling legacy products like life insurance

On Their Good Behavior

Personally, I'm sorry to say that in my businesses, the best-behaved customers overall are in Canada and the U.K., not here at home in the U.S. Our audiences here, for example, have ants in their pants, are up and down and in and out of the room during a presentation, must be browbeaten to turn off their cell phones, and think little of leaving early, but Canadians and Brits think of all this as rude. I've had doctors compare notes, and the ones practicing in U.S. major cities suffer a much higher rate of no-shows and last-minute cancellations than do the doctors in Canada, the U.K., and some other countries. However, there is profound age bias to this, at least in the U.S., and the LEB/S consumer is far more likely to be well-behaved than are younger consumers. I recognize, in making this observation, I can easily be accused of displaying my own bias of age, of being a grumpy old man. I can only assure you that I work at objectivity on this point. When my wife Carla and I go to a performance at the Cleveland Playhouse, I pay attention to the percentage dressed appropriately or inappropriately, in their seats ahead of time or arriving late, in each age group. I do the same thing at the seminars and conferences where I speak or that I host. In businesses where I have access to data, I investigate refund rates by customer age groups. In various other ways, I try to take an emotionally distanced approach, and I am convinced that the likelihood of customers being on their best behavior rises dramatically with LEB/S. I also believe the differences in good vs. bad behavior between age groups are widening and growing more stark.

When LEB/S customers are given "the rules," and given good reason for them, and benefit by adhering to them, they generally follow them. I happen to be a big advocate of doing business on your own terms, and of having certain well-defined and communicated rules of engagement for how your clients are to interact with you. At seminars, I always begin with what the creator of EST, Werner Erhard, called "The Agreements Process," so that the attendees clearly know what constitutes good behavior and what is expected of them. With my one-to-one client relationships, the same sort of communication occurs in writing and at the meeting in which they are accepted as clients. If you read my book, *No B.S. Time Management for*

Entrepreneurs, you'll find a lot more detail about this. I've long taught chiropractors the strategy of communicating desired patient behavior with both an agreements process within their sales presentation (typically called "report of findings") and by promoting competition for Patient of the Month honors, which requires: 1) Keep all your appointments; 2) Show up on time; 3) Be compliant (do the assigned at-home exercises, etc.); 4) Refer new patients who we can help. I teach everybody that clients, customers, or patients are very, very bad things to have, if you have poor control over their behavior! And I do *not* believe that good behavior occurs by happy accident.

Their Charitable Nature, Your Opportunity

LEB/S donors very disproportionately support America's charities, academic and medical institutions, the arts, churches, and causes. For every dollar the rest of the population gives, they give ten. There is some variance by the nature of the nonprofit, but not much. Charities are very vulnerable to the failure of replacement spending/giving of demographic groups following LEB/S.

My client, Nelson Searcy, pastor of the famous ministry The Journey, and a consultant and coach to churches and pastors nationwide, specializes in helping churches grow younger congregations, and one of the things he has to do is guide the pastors in aggressively teaching and training their flocks to be charitable; it's not in their conditioned behavior. To this end, he supplies books like *The Generosity Ladder*, sermons, audio CDs and DVDs. (You can see his work at www.churchleaderinsights.com.)

LEB/S are different. They were raised to give, are conditioned to give, and they are experienced givers. They've also had sufficient time to become interested in and involved with supporting certain charities and charitable activities. This provides great opportunity to any business that will link itself to a charity popular with a particular audience, especially via direct-mail campaigns.

This is an under-utilized strategy, available to both national and local marketers. Shopping for and securing the appropriate donor lists is key, and if you need guidance about that, or about anything involving mailing lists, I recommend connecting with Craig Simpson at www.simpson-direct.com.

Of course, at the local community level, there are often local institutions popular with just about everybody. My long-time student, Dr. Gregg Nielsen, a very successful small-town chiropractor, regularly runs new-patient promotions linked to fundraising for the town's fire department or its food bank.

It is good to be charitable, and to use your business and its marketing to support good charities, causes, and projects. It makes a good impression on LEB/S consumers. It can be used tactically, directly, in advertising, direct-mail, and other marketing.

Cloning of Good Customers

Just about every merchant, service provider, or professional knows a referred prospect is more likely to buy, and less price or fee resistant than a prospect created cold from advertising or marketing. I agree, even though I make my living from advertising and marketing. If everybody started getting all the referrals they should and could get, were it their number one priority, I'd quickly be forcibly retired. I exist largely because of systemic failures in this area.

One of the things most businesspeople don't think about is the comparative quality and value of different customers, by source or demographics or other basis, by which discriminatory marketing could be conducted. Most are very democratic. *Any* customer is just fine. It is incredibly stupid to invest this way. It'd be like a farmer paying the same for certified black angus cows, mongrel cows of poor breeding, cows of any age, etc., buying 'em sight unseen by the truckload. You want to exercise some control over the herd you assemble. If, for example, it costs you $200.00 to get a customer from one source but only $50.00 to get one from another source, if you're a dummy, you'll refuse to use the first source and get all your customers from the second, without bothering to calculate their long-term or total customer value, the frequency with which they purchase, whether they buy at full price or only buy discounted promotional offers, whether or not they refer, and without considering how they behave. If the customer acquired for $50.00 is only worth $120.00, but the customer acquired for $200.00 is worth $650.00, then you'd be making a big mistake, in terms of dollars or percentages. Very, very, very few businesspeople track the referral propensity of different customers acquired differently, from different sources, or of different ages, genders, geography. They should, and many would be surprised if they did, but they don't.

I can tell you, broadly, that LEB/S customers have a greater propensity for referring and better ability to refer good customers than customers in other demographic groups. They are more able because they are more likely centers of influence or in leadership roles in groups or communities, they are more listened to and respected by peers, and they have access to and influence with potentially good customers who are their clones. They are more likely because they better appreciate expertise, quality, good service, and good results. In short, the more you focus on doing business with LEB/S consumers, the easier a time you'll have cloning your customers through referrals.

These ten advantages of marketing to the LEB/S market have financial ramifications. They connect to price elasticity and profitability, the amount you can afford to invest in customer acquisition and to retention, and the sustainability and value of your business.

CHAPTER 10

Avoid the Hazards with Frame-of-Reference Marketing

Dan Kennedy

There are six specific hazards in communicating with and building trust with LEB/S. Stepping in any one of them, even a little, can sabotage an entire marketing campaign or sales presentation with everything else in it done perfectly. Here are the six sandtraps to watch out for on the course:

1. Disrespecting their heroes
2. Disagreeing with their predetermined beliefs
3. Missing their frame of reference
4. Hearing what they say but missing what they mean
5. Disrespect (perceived disrespect)
6. Misaddressing their reasons for reticence

Who Are Their Heroes?

LE-boomer women name Oprah Winfrey more often than anyone else. If asked to name a broadcast personality, the majority of LE-boomer men name Rush Limbaugh, although Howard Stern registers on the list. Overall, Ronald Reagan wins this derby. Then, of course, there are subsets. Ultraconservatives will name Reagan, but also broadcasters like Glenn Beck and Mark Levin.

Seniors who are Catholic almost always name the Pope, but LE-boomers, even Catholics, rarely do.

So, assume you are a financial advisor, and your prospect brings up the matter of gold. Because you genuinely believe it is a poor investment (and because you sell annuities), you quickly cite the case against it, and emphasize your point by criticizing the "gold peddlers" on the radio like Glenn Beck. Now suppose your prospective client owns gold, bought because he is a committed Glenn Beck listener. Who wins this clash of titans—you or Glenn Beck?

These are the kind of land mines waiting for you to step on them.

Disagreeing brashly with LEB/S's predetermined beliefs is just as dangerous as disrespecting their heroes. In the 2012 presidential race, for example, you can't assume your conservative Republican client is for Romney. Some evangelical Christians and some Catholics devoutly, firmly believe that the Mormon faith is not a Christian faith, and will not set that aside to support Mitt Romney. You cannot assume your wealthy couple with four adult children is keenly interested in legacy and estate issues; that is no longer a universal belief of seniors, and certainly not of LE-boomers.

As a matter of fact, it's a bad idea to assume anything. This book gives you considerable insight into the mindset of the LEB/S consumer, drawn from research as well as the extensive experience Chip and his clients in the LEB/S health-care industry and that I and my diverse clients have marketing to these consumers most successfully. You, of course, have your own experience and your own ideas. It is all worth about as much as a tablespoon of warm spit until it is validated in actual use, marketing your business to your target audience. But in advance of that acid test, you can and should test your premises, ad copy, and other marketing with as low cost, small-ball as possible, via surveys, polls, informal focus groups conducted with a handful of your best customers, direct attempts at selling face to face or to small groups brought together for that purpose, as well as split tests of headlines, offers, prices, etc., via online and offline media. For consumers, I'm a fan of split tests in Val-Pak, 5,000 coupons with "A" and 5,000 with "B" to the same zip code; the same done with postcards; the same done via Google AdWords.

Oops, You Missed It by *That Much*!

If you are of a certain age, that phrase is within your ready frame of reference and may have brought forth a little smile. It's one of Don Adams' catch-phrases from the spy spoof TV show, *Get Smart*.

It's important to know and understand the frame of reference of your LEB/S consumer.

Formative experiences for the LE boomer include the Cold War and nuclear annihilation threat, the Civil Rights movement, the Vietnam War, the draft and the end of the draft, the anti-war movement, assassination of JFK, RFK, and Martin Luther King, Jr., the sexual revolution, and Watergate. It is easy for me to rattle these off, because they're my frame of reference. I remember the hide-under-your-desk drills at school. I can recall where I was when JFK was shot. I definitely recall Watergate. I would like to have been more of a beneficiary of the sexual revolution than I was. I lived close to Kent State. I campaigned for McGovern. The war ended shortly before my number would have come up in the draft, and there was talk in my anti-war (but otherwise fairly conservative) household of moving to Canada. Many boomers who are entrepreneurs like me have very vivid recollections of coping with the Jimmy Carter recession's trifecta: triple-digit inflation, interest rates, and unemployment while beginning our business careers.

Many LE-boomers were all about achievement with a capital A, thus optimism, competitiveness, being defined by careers, workaholism, and visible success have been important drivers in their lives. Others were idealistic and stayed liberal well into adult years, although most LE-boomers are now conservative.

This information tells you how to form effective selling relationships with them. They want to see that you are working hard for them, because they value hard work. They want to know that you are accomplished and recognized for your accomplishment, because they value accomplishment and recognition.

Seniors obviously have different formative experiences. I know that for my parents, the way of life begun immediately after World War II and the Big Band Era were touchstones. I'm not going to go into more detail here; if you are not a senior, you have parents or grandparents to talk to, you can do research. I can tell you that the WWII experience made this the most patriotic of all generations, so, in forming selling relationships with seniors, especially military veterans, authentic displays of patriotism foster trust.

The "2010 Del Webb Boomer Survey" produced interesting lists of celebrities with which different age groups most closely identified. In declining order, the 50-year-olds identified with:

- Oprah
- Sandra Bullock

- Julia Roberts
- Ellen DeGeneres
- Jennifer Aniston
- Valerie Bertinelli

I find it suspicious that all named were women, but it should not go unnoticed that DeGeneres, Aniston, and Bertinelli have all been tapped for more than one advertising campaign aimed at boomer women.

The 64-year-olds identified with:

- John Wayne
- Clint Eastwood
- Sally Field
- Oprah
- Bill Cosby
- Meryl Streep

Frame of Reference is built with WHO, WHAT, WHEN, and WHERE. For Jewish LEB/S who grew up in the East, the Catskills is a powerful WHERE reference, from their summers. For seniors, Martin & Lewis, and Frank Sinatra are powerful WHO references; for LE-boomers, the Beatles and the Rolling Stones are more so. My LE-boomer friend has a shirt that reads: I May Be Old, But At Least I Saw The Best Bands. The other night, at a dinner table with several seniors and several LE-boomers, their familiarity with "party line" phones, wall phones, a home having one or at most two phones (the wall phone in the kitchen, the main phone in the foyer on its own stand), and the first portable briefcase phones was explored. Automobiles of peoples' youth are very powerful WHAT references, more for men than women. At the end of this chapter, I've reprinted a few pages from my autobiography, about my cars. I use this sort of material to deepen the bond with my readers, fans, customers, clients, and

GKIC members. Judging from the mail I get, sometimes with old photos of their cars, and the conversations that start with them telling me their car stories, I know this has impact.

I coach business owners in incorporating positive emotional anchors that fit their customers' fondest frame of reference—early childhood through high school graduation—into their office environments, their advertising and marketing, and their personal storytelling.

It's also important to keep the LEB/S's financial frame of reference from that time period in mind. He likely remembers the price paid for his first car (mine was $3,990.00), the rent

FIGURE 10.1

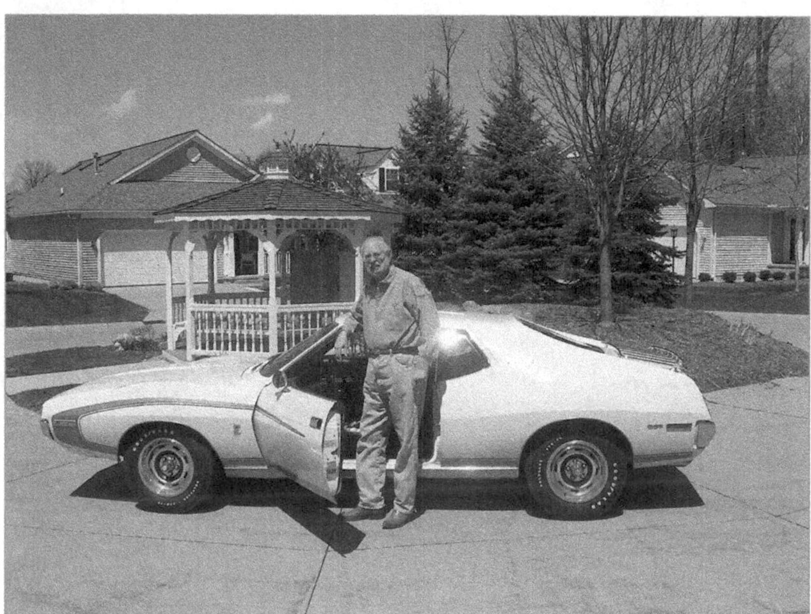

This is a 1972 AMC Javelin AMX, with a Pierre Cardin interior, that I bought, restored, for $39,995.00. The 1973 Javelin that I bought for myself brand-new from the dealership cost me $3,990.00. If I only knew then what I know now, I'd have bought two and cocooned one!

on his first apartment, price of gas, loaf of bread, movie ticket, postage stamp. These are fixed in place, and as LEB/S age, they are increasingly likely to recall these prices and compare what they are currently being asked to pay for something—vocally or silently—to the nostalgia price. It may be an odd quirk, but it is very common. Price is always "felt" in more than one context, not just weighed against value. Of course, nobody expects to pay the 1950, 1960, or 1970 price for anything, but the quick lurch of the comparison can give somebody pause. But this represents a broader point about frame of reference: the life and times of your customer—from birth to high school; driver's license; first car; first romance; college or military service; first jobs; marriage and first child—implant vivid memories, some fondly held, some not, that influence current thinking and buying behavior. All this offers great opportunity to the adept marketer or sales professional to create emotional affinity, a higher and deeper and more influential form of rapport.

Did You Hear What He Said or What He Meant?

In reviewing transcripts from recordings of actual conversations between the salespeople in hearing-aid centers and the customers, I was dumbstruck by one; by how badly the salesman had missed his cue. It had gotten to price. The customer, a 70-ish gentleman, raised it simply, "Well, just how much are these things, anyway?" This telegraphs he has resigned himself to needing them and is ready to buy, even if not with happy enthusiasm, and that's a good thing. The salesman then baldly stated a price that was met with sticker shock. The customer said, slowly, "Gee, I really wasn't prepared to spend that kind of money on myself." The salesman instantly launched into a regurgitation of a memorized spiel already used once, justifying the value against the price, citing how it was made, the sophistication of the technology, the warranty. And he whiffed. Because the customer had NOT objected to the price nor questioned the value. Were I in that salesman's place, I'm very confident I would have heard what the customer meant, and been able to navigate my way to giving him the permission he needed, to making the purchase okay. I would have asked a couple questions to learn he was a widower with grandchildren, and gotten to the fact that, at this stage of life, he felt most concerned with leaving them as much of his money as he could, to give them the best leg up in life possible. I could then have made the points that money left behind isn't the only and maybe not the best way to assist the grandkids; that being able to be fully engaged with them, to hear them clearly and respond well, to point out the call of a bird during a walk, to read a story, to be trusted to take them on outings might matter as much; that his family would surely agree that he had worked hard his whole life and done his level best at raising his family, and had earned and deserved the best hearing possible, for his own safety and security as well as for their benefit in enjoying their time with him. I would have steered the conversation there, not into the palladium sensors with NASA technology, or the 60-month payment plan.

I once spent a week masquerading as a grandson of a rented elderly lady, playing prospects, taking tours and meeting with salespeople at retirement communities in Florida, and I found the same missing of cues occurring.

Seniors are not often direct about their financial or emotional concerns. What appears to be a price objection will be raised as a red herring, masking the person's real thoughts of the moment. Even LE-boomers can be reticent in such disclosures to strangers. In advertising, marketing, and selling by media, we don't even get cues. We communicate one way with no feedback. The cues must be imagined and anticipated, understood through research and insight, and raised and addressed. Even a baby elephant ignored in the room will block a sale.

I Don't Get No Respect

This boomer reference is the catch line of the late Rodney Dangerfield. Boomers know him from his late-career work in films and LE-boomers may know him more, and seniors definitely know him from his nervous, sweaty, stand-up comic appearances on all the popular TV shows, continuing throughout Johnny Carson's tenure, in which Rodney complained bitterly, via one-liners, of all the disrespect shown him by his parents when a child, girls he dated, his wife, and the world around him.

LEB/S can't stand disrespect. We believe we've earned respect. Some of us react rather violently; I'm not proud of it, but I have been removed by security guards from both a Best Buy and a Kohl's store, after I delivered rather forceful lectures on respecting elders and the customers actually signing all the paychecks to snot-nosed, disdainful young punks. Very recently, I leapt up from a restaurant table in front of friends, found the owner, and demanded a different wait person replace the extremely disrespectful and disagreeable young girl who had raised my ire. No LEB/S likes disrespect. Most feel it profoundly. Most don't make a scene over it, they just make a note of it, and take their business elsewhere, while telling a dozen other people of being treated poorly.

Seemingly little things can be big irritants, just as in all marketing, little hinges can swing open big doors. One of the top three complaints of LEB/S patients about doctors' offices and hospitals is being called (yelled at) by a nurse at a distant door, to "come on back," made worse when they use just a first name in place of Mr. or Mrs. The winning procedure is for the nurse to walk to the waiting patient and quietly and courteously invite them to accompany her. A common customer nonservice complaint I hear when I quiz LEB/S consumers about disrespect is having a business's phone answered, the person hastily saying, "I have to put you on hold," and doing so. Over half say when it happens and they are calling to place a take-out order, they hang up and just cook something; over one-fourth say if calling a new service provider, say a plumber, and it happens, they hang up and move on to the next Yellow Pages ad. My co-author of the book *Uncensored Sales Strategies* and a consultant on exceptional customer experiences, Sydney Barrows (www.SydneyBarrows.com), did an extensive research project on cosmetic surgery practices and their patients, and discovered that LEB/S patients felt having to deal with "excruciatingly young" staff in the office was a sign of disrespect by the doctor! And, while it might not derail their relationship, it would preclude referrals.

LEB/S also quickly form and carry grudges. I'm Irish and our old-age joke is about Irish Alzheimer's. You forget everything but your grudges. There will be a price exacted for perceived disrespect: a warm prospect suddenly turned cold and unresponsive, a customer lost, negative word-of-mouth. If you are to succeed with the LEB/S clientele you choose and target, you need to give a lot of thought to how you can show respect, and how you might err and show disrespect; to staffing with people trained and coached in this and, ideally, with affinity to the clients; and in policing the procedures you settle on.

I'd Rather Fight Than Switch

Do you recognize that ad slogan? LEB/S will. And it speaks to their reticence about switching from the familiar to the unknown.

Loyalty is a value prized by LEB/S. They are reluctant to leave the professionals and service providers they've had long relationships with, or to "cheat on" the restaurants and retail shops they've long patronized. In this way, selling to LEB/S has a lot of commonality with B2B marketing and selling, where you are always trying to disentangle a purchasing agent or business owner from the existent vendor relationship. There is loyalty and obligation. There is also risk of the new, even when barely satisfied with the present. Seniors also have fealty to existent trust and authority figures.

LEB/S also have loyalty to ways of conducting business. In our area, an upscale grocery chain with several stores in affluent LEB/S areas continues to provide "bag boys" who carry the bags out to the curbside and load them into the trunk or back seat for the customer. This, many of these consumers believe, is the way it's supposed to be. That's key: ***What is their belief system about the way something is supposed to be or be done?*** There is opportunity in being the last business standing with an established, accepted *modus operandi*. There is a challenge that can't be underestimated in attempting to switch LEB/S to a new and different way, particularly if it's perceived as a downgrade in customer service. Netflix got a very dramatic lesson in this in 2011, when it attempted to separate its DVD delivery service from its online system and charge extra for access to DVD delivery: Customers left in a news-making stampede. Supermarkets and airlines had hoped to completely eliminate cashiers and ticket agents by now in favor of self-checkout and kiosks, and online check-in, but the LEB/S consumers have resisted to such an extent that the pace of forced change slowed to a crawl. Service as we've known it (and millions of service jobs) will be erased and replaced with self-service and online-only service as time marches on, predominately by entire industries acting in concert so that the consumer has no options, but when any marketer breaks ranks, there's trouble. Ally Bank, an "online bank" intended to operate with the internet as its only door, is, as I write this, ever more aggressively advertising the fact that customers can phone and get connected to a human 24/7.

FIGURE 10.2: Frame-of-Reference WHAT Example

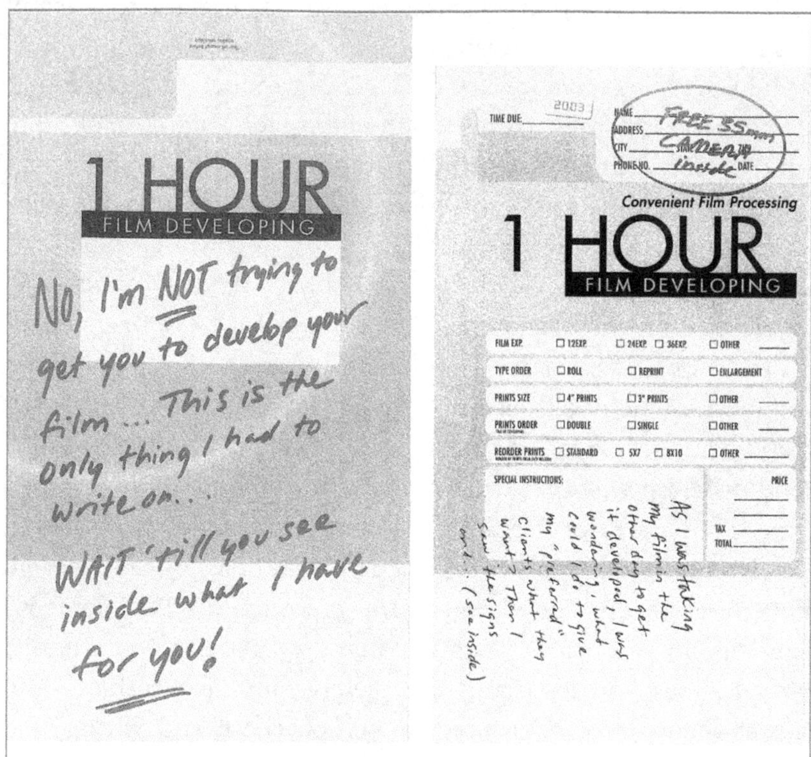

Here's a Frame-of-Reference WHAT, known to LEB/S: a "replica" film-for-developing envelope used as an envelope for sales material.

Excerpt from Unfinished Business

A man may not remember the day or month or even the year he met his wife, may not remember old girlfriends' names. Forget all sorts of things about people. But he can recall every car and every detail about every car, and the distance of time breeds nostalgic fondness for the cars of the past, the cars of our youth. Especially the first car. I even remember the little white plastic doohickey on the key ring, imprinted in faded gold lettering, advertising a tavern that was out of business.

My first car was a 1960 Chevrolet Impala, and it was not 1960. I bought it for $50.00. $25.00 down, $5.00 a month. It was turquoise, blue and white, white roof, huge fins. It had over 100,000 miles on it and had not aged well. The floor was patched with license plates. In wet or winter weather, water and slush squirted up through holes in the floor. The roof leaked. One window sagged and wouldn't stay all the way up. There was a lot of rust. But by far its biggest flaw was the rear frame, rusted through and cracked on both sides, past the rear wheels. So the long trunk and fins were held up by frames wrapped in wood blocks (from a set of blocks I'd had as a kid, that had been my Dad's when he was a kid) and duct tape, then wired and turnbuckled forward to a more solid part of the car. This meant you could not jack up the car to change a rear tire; it had to be towed to a gas station with an x-frame. And you couldn't put weight in its trunk. It had bald tires. I'll say this for her, she always started. Parked outside in frigid weather, covered in snow, she still always started. Certainly can't say that about any woman I've ever been involved with. And, in ratio terms, I've never made as good an investment. I drove her for over a year, added nearly 50,000 miles, and ultimately

Excerpt from Unfinished Business

got $25.00 for her when she died—and I took out and kept the eight-track player.

This Chevy died in a heart-wrenching way, which I describe later in this book.

It deserved a gentler demise, a gracious retirement. It didn't get one.

I have a little metal model of her in my home.

Next, my JFK Lincoln. A huge boat of a car. Battleship gray 1964 Town Car with suicide doors. Its body had seen better days, the steering was so sloppy you had to turn the wheel around twice to make a sharp turn. I only paid $300.00 for it, so no shame. It did have a big eight-cylinder engine, lots of power, lots of speed. I drove her all over my five-state sales territory for four months while waiting for my company car. I also recall picking up a girl for a first date in the Lincoln. It was a long driveway. Halfway to the street, the girl made an unkind comment about the car. By the time I got to the street, I'd made my decision. I put her out there and drove off.

This car was so heavy that, once it was moving, it had so much momentum I once ran out of gas coming down the off ramp of the Ohio Turnpike at Exit 11 and coasted all the way down the ramp, onto Route 21, down that highway into the gas station.

It was so long and big and bulky, I once got it wedged in a circular exit from a parking garage in Columbus, Ohio. Right front fender, left rear fender, stuck.

The brand spankin' new company car provided by my one and only employer, Price/Stern/Sloan, was a 1974 Chevelle Malibu Classic, maroon, white top. My first new car. And sadly, not much of a car. In eight months working for P/S/S, it needed

Excerpt from Unfinished Business

two transmissions replaced. Its ride never recovered from my girlfriend nearly totaling it the second week I had it, while I was out of town in L.A., at the company sales meeting. It wasn't easy explaining how I did $6,000.00 damage to this car when I wasn't there. Ultimately, its final moment with me was a bitter, bitter cold, subzero morning in Grand Rapids, Michigan, when I unfroze the door lock, opened the door, and had its hinges crack in half. Driving from Grand Rapids home to Cleveland with the driver's-side door in the back seat and snow swirling in all over me—and being stopped three different times by the highway patrol—was a life-changing event. As soon as I got home, I called the office and quit.

I immediately bought my own new car, a 1974 American Motors Javelin, flame red, white racing stripes, white bucket seats, black interior, white top. I loved this car. I'd love to have one now. I smashed it up pretty good on a little trip to Murray, Kentucky, described elsewhere in this book.

I traded what was left of the Jav in for a new 1975 Mercury Cougar. That model was the same as the Lincoln Mark IV. A big, long hood. Maybe the best car I ever owned.

I was still living at home, but spending a whole lot of time at the Akron apartment of the slightly older divorcee I later married. One night, driving home very late, slightly drunk, I dozed off at the wheel and the car banged its way along the side of a cliff, against a guard rail until I woke up from the thump-thump-thump and screaming, scraping. The passenger side of the car was ground meat.

That morning I traded what was left of the Cougar in on a 1976 Olds Cutlass Supreme, silver and black.

Excerpt from *Unfinished Business*

That car was repossessed.

Two days after it was repo'd, I leased a 1978 Lincoln Continental Town Car, a magnificent beast. An odd metallic rose color, maroon top, maroon interior. That's the car I drove to Phoenix in, and had there until it was repossessed.

Two cars repossessed in one 12-month span. Not good.

I briefly had a really old, bad Cadillac on weekly payments from a tote-the-note lot.

I briefly drove a friend's Pontiac TransAm, the *Smokey and the Bandit* car, gold with black firebird on hood, pop-out glass roof. The engine idled at 40 miles an hour. I got two speeding tickets the same day. Actually, in the same hour. Two neighboring communities. All within four miles. Then, a good, used Cadillac. Then, a brand-new Lincoln.

From there forward it doesn't matter much. Cars don't matter at all to me now. But I miss my '60 Chevy, my '64 Lincoln in spirit. I don't miss driving around on bald tires in leaking, rusty, dangerous cars. But I miss them in spirit. I miss my Javelin, my Cougar, my rose-colored Lincoln. I miss my youth, which has disappeared right along with the cars. I miss the fumbling, figuring-it-out-as-I-went sex that occurred in several of those cars. I miss the ability to be joyous and excited and superior and powerful just from getting behind the wheel of a brand-new car.

Now that I think about it, maybe I'll go buy a car.

Note: This chapter was written before I acquired the classic cars I now own. I guess it was a sales letter to me.

CHAPTER 11

The Power of the Right Media Strategy:

The Online vs. Offline Debate and the LEB/S Market

Dan Kennedy

Marketers are understandably very, very eager to abandon offline media in favor of online media. Many marketers are also greatly influenced by young advertising and marketing agency leaders and "gurus." Unfortunately, the actual experience of people "on the ground," most successfully selling to LEB/S, as well as the facts obtained from close examination of their results, commands us to stay focused on, and to weight our marketing investments to, offline media.

Here are some very telling facts, drawn from some thorough (and very expensive) research done by an outside, objective team of analysts for a multimillion-dollar producer in the financial services field, marketing to modestly affluent to very affluent LEB/S clients, in 2011, courtesy of my co-author of the

No B.S. Trust-Based Marketing book, Matt Zagula. Clients were interviewed to determine how they were sourced and how the financial firm first came to their attention and garnered their interest. Thirty-four percent cited word of mouth—conversations with family, friends, or peers—out of which came a specific recommendation or proactive referral. Nearly the same, 33%, cited the firm's offline media advertising and direct mail for its public, educational seminars and workshops, prompting attendance as response. In specific response, there was overlap: People responding to advertising and attending events also had conversations with peers in which the firm was favorably mentioned. Conversations with peers were also prompted by the events themselves, with attendees not converting to clients still positively influencing others. Another 15% cited the firm's non-event-related media exposure, including advertising on radio and TV and in newspapers, as well as its principals heard or seen interviewed on radio and TV. **Significantly, no one cited any online media as the starting point of their move to relationship with the firm. *No one. Nada. Zero*.**

That should be disturbing to anyone in the financial services field devoting a significant portion of their ad budget, marketing resources, or personal or staff time to online media, notably including social media. Arguably, if it produces 0, it deserves 0%. That would be overly extreme, of course, because *some* presence is essential for credibility if and when potential clients go online at some point, and for the media, and there are things that can be done online to educate prospective clients during and after the sales process, online workshop registration options can be offered, webinars promoted to unconverted leads, and so forth. But to invest in online media as if it was a productive driver of new business is, based on these facts, foolhardy. This cautionary note is not just for those in financial services, but for many kinds of professionals and service providers marketing to LEB/S. I know this flies in the face of a lot of statistics about the rapid growth in numbers of LEB/S using online and social media and is contrary to what you will hear from all the shovel sellers of online media shovels, including Google and Facebook themselves. But statistics are often *not* useful facts. For example, the majority of seniors and many LE-boomers have been driven to social media in order to stay in touch with their adult kids, grandkids, and distant friends, but are resistant to having their data harvested and obviously used to direct advertising messages to them, and do not go to the internet to find services and professional assistance.

As to search marketing, in which marketers invest untold sums of money, time, and energy to stay atop search engines, to build search-engine friendly content and to constantly monitor and respond to changes, it has one very big and severe flaw: It requires search. Most of my clients, in financial services, health, and other fields, make most of their money "knocking on the doors" (via direct media) of people not yet actively seeking what they offer, or even unaware it exists, or at least in circumventing and discouraging search, because search automatically creates comparison.

If we re-examine facts from this financial services firm's productive sources of clients, it tells us where and how to allocate our resources and focus our energies.

Thirty-four percent came from word-of-mouth recommendations and referrals. This suggests that 34% of our resources ought to be invested in encouraging and rewarding that client activity. This is why, in that field—with the advisors I consult with, and that Matt Zagula and I coach—we have led them to the creation and delivery of elaborate new client welcome gift packages, use of one or two monthly client newsletters (you can see the "mini-magazine" we built just for the advisors' LEB/S clients, called *Life, Liberty & Happiness,* in the *No B.S.*

Trust-Based Marketing book), special reports and white papers on different subjects offered to clients via the newsletters, periodic client appreciation events and outings, formal referral reward programs, seasonal gifting, and even more client communication and relationship tools and activities. My rule of thumb is that the client should get an offline "touch" (that is not purely a solicitation) at least 52 times a year. That will certainly include a Thanksgiving or Christmas card or card and gift, a birthday card or card and gift, a spouse's birthday card or card and gift, and at least 12 monthly newsletters. That takes care of 15, leaving 37 to be more creatively concocted.

Incidentally, this same research at this firm found that 43% of clients ranked educational events for clients as important, and 33% said that client appreciation events with a referral component, where they could bring and introduce friends in a casual, fun environment, were important. The research firm reported that as "only" 43% and 33%. I heard that one out of every three clients likes events that are fun, that they can bring friends to. I read this as an invitation to mine these clients for more referrals. As with most research, the way you ask the question matters. Only 14% responded favorably to terming these gatherings as "referral events," while 33% responded favorably to "client appreciation events."

Thirty-three percent came from the advertising for and attendance at public, educational seminars and workshops. This not only suggests at least 33% of the resources be directed there, but an expansion and creative diversification of these events to include different topics, aimed at different LEB/S segments, held in different venues, repositioned as book signings at the local bookstore and at different times of day. The combined 34% and 33% suggest great emphasis placed on getting present clients to invite and bring guests to these events.

Fifteen percent of the clients came from media advertising and media publicity, on radio, on TV, and in newspapers. This tells us where 15% of our resources should be invested.

The above research work cost a pretty penny, but I've given it to you here, free. Finding these kinds of facts in your own business, as well as observed in the practices of the most successful leaders in your field is important; acting on the facts, even more important!

"You Can't Fix Stupid!"—Ron White

Here is what I find, time and time again: direction of resources into media and marketing activity in percentages and proportions in conflict with the facts of where clients come from. In 2011, I met with a major city's food bank's marketing team, which was responsible for recruiting new donors and increasing the contributions from existent donors. Roughly 50% of their donors are LEB/S, and 70% of their contributions come from the 50%, but they have less than 25% of their resources fixated on cloning these LEB/S donors. By far, their number-one means of acquiring donors is direct mail—their least productive, social media—yet they were draining money from direct mail in order to invest hundreds of thousands of dollars into remaking their websites, producing YouTube videos, and adding an employee to manage their social media activity. I might add, there's not a single LEB/S on this team that is making all these decisions and spending all this money to attract LEB/S donors. I also talked with marketing people at one of the largest hospitals in the country, and found them in similar behavior, in conflict with their own facts, and similarly excluding LEB/S marketing professionals and advisors from their inner circle. If that strikes you as stunningly stupid, good! But take a careful look in the mirror.

A hero of many entrepreneurs is Napoleon Hill, author of the book *Think and Grow Rich*. The book, initiated at the behest of Andrew Carnegie, is a summary of 17 "laws of success" built from his in-person interviews and research with hundreds of the greatest businessmen and industrialists, inventors and entrepreneurs, and other peak achievers, in the 1917 to 1937 decades. The laws, not surprisingly, include Burning Desire and Persistence. I often point out that the one Hill cited that is *least* popular is: ACCURATE Thinking. People in advertising and marketing especially love creative thinking. They're not so fond of accurate thinking. People pushing online media as panacea and urging abandonment of offline media love innovative thinking, but they, too, are not as enthusiastic about accurate thinking. These folks love statistics that verify their own predilections but are not as passionate about useful facts that call popular ideas into question.

Google, YouTube, Facebook, et al., are powerful tools as well as fascinating toys, and they have their genuinely useful roles in marketing, and they and the next generation of online media that replace them are inarguably the future. But, contrary to Gen Xs' and Millennials' beliefs, they have not just yet *changed the world*.

If you are to successfully market to LEB/S, you must remain aware of and sensitive to *their* preferences for receiving information, for relationship communication, for advertising outreach. You must collect and consider the *facts* about *their* true behavior as consumers. You must resist the lure of the brightest, shiniest objects, and the seduction of mystics who love and promote them, instead insisting on "what works."

I am *not* claiming that various goods and services can't be marketed or merchandised via online media, online catalogs, webinars, social media, etc., to LEB/S consumers. I do it. My clients do it. I am *not* claiming that utilizing search media in marketing to LEB/S consumers is fruitless. I am *not* denying a shift in these directions. I was integrally involved in the use of online media to drive sales in excess of $1 billion in 2011. While I am, by choice, somewhat famously, *personally*, a conscientious objector to the techno-machine and a near-Luddite, refusing to own a cell phone, never activating my car's GPS, refusing to embrace the iPad, getting books from Amazon by scribbling notes on scraps of paper for my assistant, I study e-commerce and online media, I work closely with the top internet marketing wizards, I write and produce marketing for online media, and I advise companies extensively involved with online media, including those with LEB/S clientele. I am *not* standing as the last horse trader in opposition to the damn horseless carriages. But I am arguing for rational thought and proportionate investment of attention and resources based on useful facts. I am cautioning that the proliferation of online media and its popularity with younger-than-LEB/S marketers is significantly ahead of LEB/S consumers' preferences.

As a general statement, the best approach is media integration, offline/online, online/offline, offline-online-offline, online-offline-online. For example, I have a client selling prepackaged opportunities and coaching programs in real estate investing and finder's fee business operation, at entry prices as low as $149.00, up to $5,000.00. Roughly two-thirds of his buyers are LEB/S. He has made millions in recent years mailing sales letters and postcards of my devising, those driving consumers to websites where full-length sales letters as well as video presentations make the initial sale, followed by both telemarketing and more direct mail to make a series of additional sales. That's offline-online-offline. The brilliant CEO of J. Crew credits their 40 million catalogs mailed during the year as the chief driver of business to its online catalog and websites. That's offline/online. At GKIC, media like this very book push consumers to a website, where they can learn more and, at their option, engage in ongoing dialogue with me via a free trial offer claimed by instant registration online. That's offline/online (see page 264). My colleague Fred Catona, the wizard of direct-response radio (www.BulldozerDigital.com), who built giants like Priceline.com with radio, increasingly drives radio listeners to websites rather than to toll-free 800 numbers. Offline/online. I have another client very aggressively using Google AdWords and other Google media, Facebook advertising, and other social media to drive thousands of leads a week to a double-squeeze page, the second obtaining their full, hard addresses, so that an elaborate direct-mail package can be sent that sells his service. Online/offline. Comprehensive integration is the Holy Grail, so that each boat's wake lifts the other boats. However, I have just described a general marketing strategy. As soon as we narrowly target LEB/S and segments within, facts intrude that place other key objectives ahead of media integration and mandate investing resources disproportionately in certain media, and also mandate search circumvention as a chief tactic.

CHAPTER 12

The Power of Print Media and Direct Mail

Dan Kennedy

The "2011 Channel Preference Study," produced by Epsilon Targeting, a leading target-marketing research group, considered along with the "Boomer/Senior Market Study," also from 2011, commissioned by a client of mine, provides considerable verification of the vital importance of print media and direct mail in marketing effectively to LEB/S and in retaining them as customers after the first transaction, and throughout a relationship. Here are a few telling facts from that research:

- While newspapers and subscribed-to magazines rank highest in trust by LEB/S consumers, email and online media rank lowest. Overall, 26% of U.S. consumers say that direct mail is more trustworthy than email or social media, however, that number nearly doubles with LEB/S. The least trustworthy media channels are social media and blogs, achieving only 6% trust among U.S. consumers and even less with LEB/S.

- Fifty percent of U.S. consumers say they pay more attention to direct mail than they do to email, and that percentage climbs above 70% with LEB/S.
- Sixty percent of U.S. consumers say that they *enjoy* checking the mailbox for mail every day, and like receiving and opening mail, including mail about products and services of interest. This number climbs by another 10% with LEB/S consumers. Ninety-eight percent of consumers retrieve their mail from the mailbox the day it is delivered, and 77% sort through it the same day.
- Epsilon found that people had a heightened *emotional connection* with mail. A study at Bangor University, "Using Neuroscience to Understand the Role of Direct Mail," concluded that tangible materials such as direct-mail pieces trigger a much deeper level of emotional processing and generate more activity in the area of the brain associated with integration of visual and spatial information than any other media. I would point out that selling to LEB/S is very much about *emotional* connection.
- Of the small percentage of consumers who expressed preference for receiving email instead of direct mail, 34% cited "going green" and saving the environment as their primary reason. From a marketing perspective, this factor has age bias to it (more younger than older), geographic bias to it, and if using lists of direct-mail buyers, it is nearly screened out.
- Privacy is stated as an important benefit of receiving information by mail rather than via email or social media, cited

> by 37% of consumers, and again, this percentage rises to nearly 50% with LEB/S, and is also higher with product/service information in key categories such as health and financial matters. There is also a strong preference for personally addressed mail in certain categories; in financial services and insurance, for example, 31% specifically cite giving more attention and consideration to personally addressed mail.

Specific to the big daddy of social media, only 5% of consumers report regularly relying on Facebook ads for any sort of household, health, or financial services, and 33% of consumers rank ads on Facebook or other social media from "useless" to "offensive." Thirty-four percent of consumers, though, report receiving at least one "daily deal" by email from some company they have a relationship with and/or from entities like Groupon or Living Social. The LEB/S population is the fast growing user demographic for social media, but is more resistant to its use as an advertising and sales media than any other age group. Women age 50 and older are 31% more likely than those younger than 50 to click on ads on Facebook according to Social Code, yet overall usage of Facebook remains heavily weighted to young women. According to *The Media Audit,* 81% of unmarried, childless women age 18 to 34 regularly visit Facebook as well as other social media. The overall click-through statistics revealed in the week leading up to Facebook's controversial IPO were daunting to those of us in direct marketing: While Google was getting 1 in 40, Facebook was at 1 in 2000, requiring 200,000 visitors to get 100 past an ad to direct contact with an advertiser. For an advertiser converting at 10%, two million visitors are needed to make just one sale. This suggests there are many more efficient ways to invest capital, even if there are situations where the LEB/S consumer is 30% more responsive. A specific product category is also revealing: The L2 Digital IQ Index on Beauty (2011) credits Facebook with only 11% of the traffic to beauty brand websites, with 89% generated from other sources, and the top ten beauty brands (by number of fans) on Facebook have disproportionate appeal to young consumers vs. LEB/S consumers.

There is both age and gender bias with newspapers. I'm afraid the local, daily newspaper may be the first actual casualty to the digital media revolution, as readership, advertisers in number, ad revenue, and profits are in dangerous decline. As I was writing this, the city of New Orleans' newspaper announced cutting publication to just three days a week, curtailing home deliveries, and turning emphasis and hope for the future to the internet. Foolishly, many advertisers are abandoning newspapers prematurely and absent factual, sales-results based support for their decision. Other astute advertisers—particularly those aiming at LEB/S—are increasing their newspaper and newspaper free-standing insert (FSI) buys, and are able to negotiate lower rates and sometimes even appear as the only advertiser in their category.

The facts are that the LEB/S consumer regularly reads the newspaper: Over 40% read their local newspaper, front to back, three or more times per week, and over 60% read it at least once a week. LEB/S women are twice as likely as LEB/S men to read their entire local newspapers, and are slightly more than twice as likely to clip ads or remove coupons from the newspapers and respond to ads in the newspapers.

An interesting gender and affluence fact, from the Newspaper Association of America, is that 73% of women who work in professional or managerial jobs and live in households with annual incomes exceeding $100,000.00 read newspapers regularly. From my own hands-on experience with many clients and client groups in LEB/S-oriented product and service categories such as retirement-oriented financial planning, investments, implant dentistry and dentures, chiropractic care, anti-aging skin care, diet/weight-loss (for LEB/S) and other health care, the local newspaper and/or FSIs in local newspapers is the first to no worse than the third most productive and profitable advertising media used, with radio and direct mail the other two. The group of about 60 financial advisors spotted across the nation that I've provided advertising and marketing coaching to in the past couple years spends well over $10 million a year advertising in their local newspapers, increased year to year, and they should be spending more. There are very successful full-page newspaper ads bringing prospective patients to implant dentistry introductory seminars, producing from $100,000.00 to as much as $1 million a month in revenue for a single practice. Another client of mine, HealthSource, the largest nationwide franchise network of chiropractic clinics, topping 364 as of this writing, is a major user of FSIs in local newspapers in most of its markets. For as long as newspapers are available, those of us target-marketing to LEB/S consumers, especially LEB/S women consumers, need to make great use of them.

The Power of Mail-Order Catalogs

If you think catalogs are dead, the facts tell a different story. J. Crew itself mailed 40 million catalogs last year, to which it attributes drive to its website and internet sales and drive to stores; they do little other advertising. In total, more than 12 BILLION CATALOGS are mailed annually. Companies in home furnishings such as Restoration Hardware, Williams-Sonoma, and The Pottery Barn; in food such as Omaha Steaks; in apparel, such as J. Crew, as noted, and J. Peterman; in sporting goods and apparel, Orvis; in every consumer and B2B category are heavy catalog mailers. Can the management teams at *all* these companies be idiots? If they could eliminate all this expense and replace it with online media, can you think of any reason they wouldn't? They would, in a heartbeat. They can't.

LEB/S's are catalog shoppers. They buy four times as often during a year than other customers of the same catalogs and place higher dollar amount orders.

Seniors grew up with The Sears Wish Book; LE-boomers with Lillian Vernon. J. Peterman. A plethora of catalogs.

It is my contention that every business should produce and mail its own catalogs. The dental practice has multiple procedures, services, and products to showcase in its catalog: Invisalign®, implants, hygiene, tooth whitening. The restaurant has special events and seasonal menus, birthday party packages, wedding rehearsal dinners, catering. But I am especially adamant about this if marketing to LEB/S.

Good catalogs and catalog companies that are LEB/S oriented, that I recommend studying, and purchasing from in order to stay on their mailing lists to get their printed catalogs are:

- www.VermontCountryStore.com
- www.RadioSpirits.com
- www.Blair.com
- www. FirstStreet.com
- www. Orvis.com (see Figure 12.1 for an ancedote on this)
- www. FullofLife.com

You Can't Tear a Page Out of an iPad

A lot of my clients are doing very, very, very well advertising in print magazines reaching LEB/S consumers, including marketers who also extensively use online media. One to check out is www. SafetyTechnology.com, a provider of home and personal safety products, wholesale, to independent dealers, many of whom are home-based business operators. The main magazine ad I created for this company has been appearing profitably in a small

FIGURE 12.1

As an interesting side note, I bought my 1986 Jeep Wagoneer from the Orvis catalog. Right in there with the men's apparel and sporting goods.

collection of magazines every month for the past six years, driving millions of dollars of revenue. So many of their new dealers are LEB/S that the CEO, Michael Gravette, a boomer, is developing a new association, The Independent Ameri-I-Can Association, as a portal to many selected and approved home-based business opportunities (www.IndependentAmericanAssociation.com).

His is not an isolated anecdote. In every product and service category, magazine advertising is alive and well and productive with LEB/S consumers. Specialty interest magazines for hobbyists, golfers, campers, hunters, and collectors are particularly fertile. A number of direct-response advertisers targeting LEB/S do very well in the nation's Farm Bureau magazines, for which state-by-state or nationwide media buys are available. A magazine like *Entrepreneur*, published by the same company publishing this and all my No B.S. series books, continues to be a very productive ad venue for franchisors, business opportunity marketers, and small-business service advertisers. Of course, most magazines today also have robust online media, so advertisers have the ability to implement multimedia strategy.

I also have several clients who produce, publish, and distribute their own magazines. Jay Geier, the brilliant CEO of The Scheduling Institute, a consulting and training company specializing in the dental industry, publishes his own "PR" magazine, regularly published and sent to all dental practices in the U.S. that fit his geo-demographic target parameters. Although his clients span young to old, his best clients are 70% LEB/S dentists. They value receiving, read, and respond to a magazine.

Authorship Has Impact

Nothing trumps being the author of a book for credibility and authority with the LEB/S audience. Anyone can write one and everyone should. I guide just about every client I have or coach into becoming a published book author.

The Mandate

The mandate for successfully doing business with LEB/S is to effectively use print media, and use it a lot. Failure to do so puts you at odds with the communication media that they prefer, that they value, that they pay the most attention to, and that they view with the most respect.

CHAPTER 13

The Power of Fear

Dan Kennedy

While a subject that makes some queasy, the reality is that—in general—fear drives more people to action more quickly and decisively than any other motivation, and this is even truer for LEB/S.

The Power of the Hidden Fear and Benefit

In two years' intensive work consulting in the hearing aid industry and working with over 1,000 professionals in the field, and interacting with and surveying consumers, I quickly learned hidden truths about why consumers buy hearing aids.

The first thing to know is that people don't simply buy hearing aids; they *finally break down, finally give in* and buy hearing aids. A major player in the eyeglass field acquired, briefly owned, severely damaged, and subsequently sold a big hearing aid company some years back. They thought hearing aids were like eyeglasses. They were sadly mistaken. The stigma of wearing eyeglasses and the deep-seated resistance to doing so started diminishing in the 1950s and was pretty much gone by the 1970s, and today eyewear is even positioned as something you use to make a fashion statement. What helped its de-stigmatization was the fact that young people needed vision correction, so glasses were never a symbol of surrender to age and infirmity. Eyeglasses successfully moved out of the doctor's office to retail. Not so yet with hearing aids. They *are* symbolic of surrender to age. People are embarrassed by having to wear them, even now that newest technology has made them tiny, nearly invisible, and digital, thus liberated from a device for fiddling with the volume. Seen or unseen, the consumer feels old and diminished by them.

The second thing to know, a more interesting secret, is that few people buy hearing aids simply to hear better. Most of us who wear eyeglasses buy them to see better. It's a simple proposition. With vision below par and worsening, trouble reading small print or seeing signs or driving at night, we go get glasses. But the purchase of hearing aids is more complicated, and most people are not sufficiently motivated by hearing difficulties to go and buy them. Instead, there are hidden fears and hidden benefits driving this buying behavior. For example, one of the things seniors fear most is "being stuck in a nursing home." Yes, we've dressed it up for the more affluent as "assisted living." But still. Seniors want to stay in their own homes. They want to live independently. They fear my co-author, Chip Kessler's industry's nursing homes. And they fear their adult children forcing them into them. This inspires some creative and risky behavior, as seniors endeavor to conceal difficulties they are experiencing with daily life. They rightly fear their adult children's perception that they are "losing it" or "addled" or "confused," which being unable to hear properly can create. When all this is laid out for them, carefully, diplomatically, but in a way that pokes a sharp-pointed stick into these fears, the important hidden benefit of better hearing ability and quicker, more certain comprehension of conversations becomes crystal clear! For that reason, I created advertising for my hearing aid industry clients that raised this exact issue, and I taught the hearing aid professionals how to talk about it. Another hidden fear of the LEB/S beginning to experience noticeable difficulty with hearing is that their adult children will be reluctant to trust them alone with their grandchildren, especially away from home, driving about, on excursions. Being deprived of independent time with the grandchildren will strike terror into the heart of a grandmother, and at least irritate a grandfather, which makes it a useful sales tool.

I know, you've heard more than enough about the hearing aid business! But don't fall prey to ". . . but MY business is different!" theology. Virtually every business, product, and service has hidden benefits to offer linked to hidden fears of its LEB/S customers. **Age fuels fear.** As we age, capabilities are taken away from us. We start experiencing these takeaways at boomer age, we feel them accelerate and worsen as seniors. The world that was ours seems to be displaced by faster and faster change. LEB/S consumers are troubled by everything from societal, cultural and political change, to technology, to their own diminishing health, mental acuity, and vitality. Within all this anxiety, trepidation, discomfort, sometimes annoyance and even rage, and, yes, fear, lie the levers of powerful persuasive arguments.

The multibillion-dollar alternative health industry, featuring self-help health books and newsletters, common and exotic nutritional supplements, magic elixirs and tonics, lotions 'n' potions, heavily driven by direct-mail targeting LEB/S consumers is increasingly disease and infirmity specific. Boardroom, one of the largest publishers of condition-specific self-help health books and newsletters such as *Bottom Line Health* and *Bottom Line Personal,* had a blockbuster success in 2012 with a direct-mail "magalog" entirely devoted to diabetes and all its side-effect evils, selling its $39.00 book, *The 30-Day Diabetes Cure.* (Note: you can promise cure when publishing information, but not if selling ingestibles.) The publishing side of this industry has countless books, newsletters, and promotions tied to different, specific ills and cures: heart disease, cancer, joint pain and arthritis, brain fog and memory loss, irritable bowel syndrome, etc. The hidden fear within the consumers who buy frequently from many of these companies (who exchange buyer lists amongst themselves) is: getting stuck in the hospital.

Seniors know from personal and friends' experiences just how dangerous a visit to the hospital can be. They are acutely aware it all too often is the beginning of the end, and the facts bear them out. Dr. Robert Wilson, the lead author of the Chicago Health and Aging Project says, "Hospitals can be a very risky experience for the elderly. Once you get out of the hospital, your trajectory is downhill." Their study even showed a direct and dramatic link between just one multi-day hospital stay and accelerated cognitive and memory decline roughly equivalent to 10 years' instant aging! Were I writing copy for alternative health information or products with the hidden benefit of keeping you out of the hospital, I would quote Dr. Wilson. Seniors already have this fear simmering. It need only be brought to a boil to drive a sale. There are two common sort-of jokes among seniors. One has to do with skipping hospitals and nursing home and just staying on one cruise after another: It costs less, you get a private room, the food is a lot better, there's a free doctor on board, and assisted suicide or burial is available 24/7 with one dive off deck. The darker humor has to do with the pact between friends in a "pillow club." The fears of entering the hospital never to escape again, emerging so damaged that quality of life is left behind, or moved directly to incarceration in a nursing home are ever-present with many seniors.

LE-boomers are not as easily frightened by the specters of endless hospitalization and torture to death as are seniors, but they are just as susceptible to the alternative investment industry's pronouncements of impending economic Armageddon. In 2011 and through 2012, friends of mine in the newsletter business at the giant publishing house, Agora, brought on nearly one million new subscribers with their now iconic EndOfAmerica.com campaign, featuring dark-toned, somber-voiced TV commercials, soundtrack radio commercials, and scary direct-mail booklets. Their subscriber demographic is LEB/S. (If you missed this, you can find it at YouTube. The video sales letter itself expanded to 90 minutes in length during the course of the campaign.) Chapter 17 talks more about the LEB/S financial conservatism.

The regular financial services industry benefits from sensationalism, to the extent its parent companies' compliance departments let the advisors and salespeople in the field indulge in it. My client, Matt Zagula, a seven-figure-income financial advisor, has had great success acquiring mass-affluent LEB/S clients by promoting his book, *Invasion of the Money-Snatchers: A Practical Guide to Protecting Your Stuff from Creditors, Predators, and a Government Gone Wild,* and public workshops featuring reasons to worry about changes in Medicare and Social Security, tax laws, corporate and government pensions and veteran benefits, as well as future risks of inflation to nest eggs, and solutions to all of these threats. The hidden fear he and the entire tribe of top advisors I've coached focus on is: *running out of money before you run out of years.* Many modestly affluent-to-affluent LEB/S clients rose up from humble or even poor backgrounds and/or have parents or grandparents with Great Depression memories. They are aware of the real possibility and pain of poverty. Recent national and world events have placed fears of sudden and unexpected losses on their front burners. They are sensitive to the idea they might outlive their money. Against this backdrop, the benefit of guaranteed-income-for-life financial products can take precedence over yield or appreciation. Most charities are increasingly aggressive sellers of "charitable annuities" that guarantee set income for life to the donor (plus tax benefits), but take the principal out of the person's estate and give it to the charity, sometimes to the distress of potential heirs. This entire business is fueled by the fear of outliving one's money.

On the Other Hand, There Are Fears in the Way

LEB/S consumers have definite fears that interfere with selling to them. These fears all center around making mistakes.

Seniors become increasingly sensitive to and concerned about embarrassment as they age: doing something that proves to be foolish; being taken advantage of; opening themselves up to criticism by family and close friends; or, worse, the idea circulating among family and friends that they can't take care of themselves, can't manage their money, can't be trusted without supervision. Seniors are also painfully aware they lack the luxury of time to recover and rebound from mistakes. If their earning years are past or soon to be over, they lack the ready capability of replacing money lost, and they know it. This aids my clients in the financial arena selling investments with high safety but very low yield, because their clients are far more concerned with preservation of principal than they are gains. It stands firmly in the way of those selling speculative or relatively unusual investment products. This fear, like most, is a double-sided coin, with gold on one side, tin on the other.

LE-boomers are not so sensitive to elapsed time and limited remaining years, and may not be as sensitive to criticism either, but they are still growing more risk averse and certainly concerned with each passing day. They, too, *can* be scared.

CHAPTER 14

The Power of Familiarity

Dan Kennedy

For many, many years Paul Harvey was *the* market-maker for advertisers, the millionaire-maker for many entrepreneurs, especially those selling to 55-and-overs. His endorsement within commercials almost seamlessly woven into his news and commentary drove sales, delivered customers, built companies. Why was his word so powerful? Because he was so very, very familiar. He was invited into homes and listened to every day, often talked about at the evening dinner table. Cronkite was dubbed "the most trusted man in America," but if you judge that by sales impact, you'd award the title instead to Paul Harvey. They had much in common. Paternal, gently authoritative, elder statesmen of sorts. Paul had the more personal relationship with his listeners than Cronkite had with his viewers. He talked to them about his thoughts and ideas, his views on national and global events, and the companies and products he discovered and liked—leaping to mind Amway and the then new-fangled Bose stereo systems. Paul Harvey was unabashedly patriotic, unabashedly enthusiastic, good-humored, just the kind of fellow a 60-year-old living in the heartland of America would love as his neighbor and trusted friend. And he dropped by for a cup of coffee every single day.

Familiarity can, as the cliché says, breed contempt. It can work against advertisers and marketers with younger consumers in lust for what's newest today, easily disdainful of or embarrassed by what is *so* yesterday. But with age, the familiar becomes more desired and appreciated, more reassuring. How many TV shows have featured the older man's *favorite* chair? Silver-haired Archie Bunker had one. Frasier's father insisted on having his planted squarely in the middle of the otherwise ultramodern, fashionably decorated living room.

It was way back in 1975 that Pepsi, frustrated with living as the perennial also-ran to Coca-Cola morphed to Coke, rolled out The Pepsi Taste Test. LEB/S will remember it well. It started as research, but for a time became a major ad campaign. It is iconic enough that, as I write this, the insurance company GEICO is satirizing it in its own TV commercial. Anyway, hundreds and hundreds of Pepsi representatives manned tables in stores and malls all throughout America as well as overseas, handing passersby two little unmarked paper cups, one with Pepsi, one with Coke. More than half the consumers expressed profound preference for Pepsi. So, wondered its executives, why the devil aren't we winning, or at least running neck 'n' neck, instead of getting outsold by Coke everywhere by a wide margin?

Years later, in 2003, Dr. Read Montague, the director of the Human Neuroimaging Lab at the Baylor College of Medicine, revisited the Pepsi Challenge, using new science. He used a particular type of MRI, with 67 test subjects. They were asked in advance about their preference for Coke, Pepsi, or neither. More than half claimed preference for Pepsi, mirroring the 1975 results. And, given the blind taste test, their brain scans verified their statements. The majority did, in fact, prefer Pepsi. But when he repeated the test with brain-activity monitoring, this time telling the 67 which brand they were drinking each time, a whopping 75% demonstrated preference for Coke. During the disclosed test, those tasting Coke had heightened activity in a different section of the brain. Dr. Montague saw a tug-of-war occurring in the brains of those who had a preference for the taste of Pepsi but knew they were tasting Coke; their rational thinking, their knowledge that Pepsi tasted better to them was trumped by their deeper emotional connections with Coke. **Deeply embedded familiarity triumphed over reason.**

You can read a bit more detail about this in Martin Lindstrom's excellent book, *Buy•ology: Truth and Lies About Why We Buy.* Lindstrom's interpretation of this science experiment is that the many, many positive associations these people had with Coca-Cola—its history, logo, colors, TV and print advertising dominant presence, maybe most importantly, their own childhood memories of Coke—over-rode their thoughtful determination that Pepsi had the superior taste. Emotional connection was the victor.

Another outstanding, very provocative book about this kind of subconscious, subliminal influence well worth reading is *The Culture Code* by Clotaire Rapaille. Its examples are not current, but don't let that distract you from its important points.

Coke benefited in 1975, in 2003, and now by being the more familiar brand. If you ask a hundred people chosen at random to name the first soft drink (or in the South, "soda pop") that leaps to mind, Coke wins. If you play the same game with a hundred LEB/S consumers Coke wins by a bigger margin. I can't count the number of times I've been in restaurants with different people and listened as they ordered a Coke and were told *apologetically* by the waitperson that they *only* had Pepsi. The customer almost always shrugs and accepts Pepsi. Sometimes they even comment that the Pepsi tastes good, or even better than the Coke they wanted. Presumably if they were involved in a blind taste test, they would choose Pepsi. But it's a safe bet, the next time they sat in a restaurant and were asked what they'd like to drink, the first thing to leap to mind would still be Coke. And they would do just the same, facing the Coke and Pepsi on supermarket or convenience store shelves. It is significant that there is an enormous amount of licensed Coke merchandise—apparel, glassware, collectible figurines, Norman Rockwell art, toys, etc.—but comparatively little licensed Pepsi paraphernalia. Pepsi may win the taste test challenge, but they have lost the real test.

As a customer, as a diligent observer of marketing and business strategy, and as a shareholder, I think one of my favorite companies, Disney, has Coke's advantage, multiplied. Disney has multi-generational, deeply embedded emotional connection. What LEB/S doesn't feel fondness toward Disney? Emotional attachment to Walt, to The Mickey Mouse Club, to its most famous member, Annette Funicello? There exists in the Disney universe D23, the fraternal organization for adult, die-hard fans. If you attend D23 events, as my wife and I have, you see almost no children, few young people, a whole lot of gray hair, and a fair number of canes and walkers. You should check out D23 online at www.disneystore.com/D23 for an educational exercise in lifelong fandom.

Ironically perhaps, Playboy has much in common with Disney. It has lifelong fans, their affinity dating to the discovery and borrowing of their father's poorly hidden cache of *Playboy* magazines—a commonly shared leading-edge boomer and young-senior experience. As Playboy has suffered increasing irrelevance, given the thorough success of the sexual revolution and the proliferation of very public, readily accessible sexual images on network and cable, in virtually every magazine, heck, walking around the mall, it has survived in large part thanks to multi-generational familiarity and fondness.

It has no doubt occurred to you by now that you can't get what Coke and Disney (and Playboy!) have, in your business. Your life has limited years. Yet, my contention is that you can approximate this level of reassuring and comfortable familiarity with a much smaller, narrowed, specific target audience at a very accelerated pace, and I've worked at that with my relationship with my followers, i.e. customers and our GKIC Members, and I work with my clients and client groups to deliberately develop this for themselves with their constituencies. There are three keys:

1. Meaning
2. Frequency
3. Cultural Integration

Meaning ties many things together. For one, Frame of Reference, described in Chapter 10. Coke benefits enormously as just described from Frame of Reference. Then there's a mission or purpose for your business beyond merely being a merchant and making money. Hugh Hefner initially promoted "The Playboy Philosophy" and "What Sort of a Man Reads Playboy?", not just a magazine. Disney has a powerful origin story, a mission of bringing families together, a commitment to being "The Happiest Place on Earth." (If Walt hadn't used that line, Hef would have, for the Playboy Mansion.) There's also the matter of personal relevance and customization.

Frequency is vital. You can't be an occasional or even random visitor. Paul Harvey was there every day, Johnny

Carson every night. A LEB/S looks forward to his favorite magazines every month, rises in the morning early to walk out into his driveway and get his newspaper every day. Most who drink Coke drink it every day, although it might have been a more carefully doled out treat in childhood. If you are to have relationships with LEB/S, you must design, implement, and persist with a program of frequent friendly and interesting communication.

Cultural Integration is the ultimate prize. Although Disney makes a great deal of money from its licensed merchandise, there is just as much benefit from the integration of it all into the Disney customer's home and family life. You do not need to be in our home for very long to realize we are *serious* Disney fans. Find a room without a Mickey. We have glassware and dishes, photos and photo frames, collectibles, books, DVDs, apparel, even, in my office, a talking Disney clock: Mickey, Donald, and Goofy joyously announce each hour's arrival. Hef has traveled the same path with enough licensed Playboy merchandise and memorabilia to completely outfit a man cave. Coke has licensed apparel, collectibles, etc. I have made a big effort at achieving this for myself and for GKIC in relationships with GKIC members and my readers and clients. There are, of course, my many books, GKIC publishes five newsletters, there are wall plaques, photos and photo frames, mouse pads, coffee mugs, even a Dan Kennedy bobble head, logo and slogan apparel, and more. My goal is the same as Walt's: complete cultural integration so not a day goes by without the customer being prompted to think of me. Unlike my sources of inspiration, in my case I'm helping people *make* money, not just spend it, but I still recognize that relationship equals retention even more so than results. (Many should make a note of that. It's a million-dollar secret.)

CHAPTER 15

The Power of Stress Reduction

Dan Kennedy

Stress is the enemy of selling to the LEB/S.

Doug Hall is the founder of the Eureka! Ranch, a think tank and corporate leaders' retreat, where marketing ideas are hatched. One of the best pages in his book, *Meaningful Marketing*, presents his Data Proven Truth #61: the importance of reducing customer stress. That's worth writing down on a 4 x 6 card, in big red letters, and tacking it up where you can't help but see it, every single day.

Hall cites a study demonstrating stress's paralytic impact on thinking and decision making. Students were presented with 50 word problems to solve, with no time limit, and with free use of computers. The control group was simply asked to solve the problems. A second and third group had their hands wired to devices that they were told would deliver mild, harmless but still uncomfortable electric shocks. The second group was promised random and uncontrollable shocks. The third was promised shocks linked to their own mistake making. Participants operating without the threat of the shocks achieved near 60% success. Those under the added stress of possible electro-shocks came in at a much poorer 36% success rate. Another study of shoppers is also cited, linking their interest in shopping in different stores to their anticipation of stress and difficulty in shopping there.

All this is of multiplied significance with LEB/S consumers. Cognitive decline is exerting influence. As people grow older, they are more easily confused and overwhelmed, less certain of themselves in unfamiliar surroundings. I counsel financial advisors aiming at these clients to choose the most familiar and easily accessible sites for their public workshops, and to still include clear directions in their ads and invitations. (No, everybody does *not* use their computer or car's GPS to get directions.)

As people grow older, they experience greater anxiety about the unknown. For this reason, I have designed a LEB/S template for a brochure for financial advisors, lawyers, dentists, chiropractors, hearing-aid dispensers and other health-care professionals titled "What To Expect At Your First Appointment," that, inside, lists and explains what will happen, #1, #2, #3, beginning with something like, "#1: You will be warmly greeted by our New-Client Coordinator who will ask you a few simple questions and complete a necessary form for you. You will not be kept waiting. In fact, we don't even have a 'waiting room'!" Another page is headlined, "The Five Questions That Will Be Answered During Your Initial Appointment." This conveys value to the appointment itself, and takes away more of the uncertainty.

In situations like the hearing-aid industry, we find patients worried about being unable to afford the prescribed product, or worse, being embarrassed by having to discuss not being able to afford it with a stranger. To the senior, finances are a private matter. Self-respect and dignity are at risk. In pre-appointment literature, price isn't specifically revealed, but the fact that there are a range of prices, credit cards accepted, and easy, guaranteed finance plans requiring no approval process with payments as low as $59.00 is presented, to remove the concerns not just about affordability but about having to discuss it and having to risk the ultimate humiliation of being turned down for financing.

Stress is definitely the enemy of selling to the LEB/S. It is very likely to sabotage their ability to confidently arrive at a buying decision. But just the prospect of a stressful situation, with a pushy salesman, a difficult and confusing process, or a point of no return, is enough to stop a good prospective customer from moving toward you. The words "no salesman will call" have long been added into lead-generation advertising aimed at seniors, when possible to do so, for this reason. In my work with my clients marketing to LEB/S we usually go to more verbose and reassuring lengths in describing what will and will not occur if the prospect raises his hand and requests information. When possible, we make it clear that the customer will be in control. Also, in advertising, we strive to offer both a primary and a secondary far less threatening means of and reason for response: If the primary response desired is "come to an introductory in-office meet 'n' greet," the secondary option offered can be as nominal as, "Call our free *recorded* message and, if you like, leave your mailing information to receive a free DVD." (By offering a recorded message and automated capture, we eliminate the stress of speaking with a salesperson—who just might come through the telephone receiver and grab 'em!)

One of the gentlest, least stressful approaches to selling time shares can be experienced at the Disney theme parks and resorts, for its Disney Vacation Club. They are selling to young parents in their 30s and 40s, but also making what might be a surprising number of sales to LEB/S consumers. Throughout the parks, there are staffed kiosks, and at the resort properties with a Vacation Club building, there is an open model unit, staffed, but not hawkishly guarded. Guests can chat with the representatives at the kiosks or at the models casually. The reps are trained to stay relaxed, answer questions, let the guest guide the conversation and its pace. The offer is to arrange for pickup and transport to the Vacation Club Center to meet with a sales representative, but it is made as gently as if attempting to hand-feed a tidbit to a deer. Of course, there is the very helpful benefit of being Disney (see Chapter 14). Still, for what is typically a stressful situation for a prospect, they have eased the stress all they can. The face-to-face meeting in the "closing room" (i.e., torture chamber) with the salesperson is also gentled. I've been the target of a lot of time-share pitches myself over the years—as prospect and as mystery shopper—and I've never experienced any so casually relaxed as the one Carla and I got from our DVC rep, Tony Heard. I tested him, throwing up little roadblocks to the sale to which he might have responded aggressively. He ignored the bait. And we bought, never once feeling pressured. I'm a good buyer, that's true, but then so are most LEB/S consumers in the proper environment.

I tell everybody they should "play prospect" and experience the Disney Vacation Club sales process even if they have no interest in ownership, as a great educational experience. Tony and the rest of the sales team might not appreciate my encouraging disinterested prospects to use them this way, but I reiterate the recommendation nonetheless. And I do know of three who went just to see the performance and wound up buying.

Here's what's challenging for you: It's difficult for you to see yourself as scary or intimidating, difficult for you to see your sales process as stressful for your customers. Hospital administrators, staffs and doctors are burdened with this difficulty. They can't really grasp how much people stress out in deciding to go, in going, in arriving. It'll be difficult for you as well. After all, what you do is normal and routine to you. You can't imagine that, like a startling bogeyman, *you* are raising your prospects' stress level. You can't equate *your* office or showroom to a little house of horrors, but what's safe as safe can be to you is just that—a house of unknown and worrisome bogeymen to your customer, client, or patient.

Such stress is best diffused in advance of their visit but also by a congruent, carefully crafted and choreographed experience for them when they do visit. My friends at Gardner's Mattress do an exceptional job with both, described by them in Chapter 22.

In many ways everything described in this book, and all the demonstrations in the example case histories in chapters yet to come have been about reducing customer stress and achieving all of its opposite states, including comfort, sense of affinity, respect, being understood, safety and security, and more. The goal is to make the entire process for the LEB/S customer stress-free, for him to be as comfortable and secure with you as with a trusted friend, with your place of business as with his own home.

CHAPTER 16

The Power of Differentiation

Charles W. Martin, DDS, MAGD, DABOI, DICOI, FIADFE, CEEE

As products and services become increasingly alike in features and benefits, potential buyers look for other ways to discern differences among offerings. Who you are, what you stand for, and why you do what you do become more important as a way of creating a difference where no discernable difference stood before.

From the perspective of the uninitiated, your offerings can look amazingly like everyone else's in the marketplace. So what is a buyer to do? <u>They look for differences</u> they can use to justify their decisions rationally and emotionally. While the emotional differences weigh the most heavily, the rational ones are the ones they use with family, friends, and co-workers to justify decisions. Not having these "reasons why" readily available for them to use does you and your offering a disservice and handicaps the decision-making process you have worked so diligently to ensure that it go smoothly!

While the most effective differentiators are the differences that matter to your targeted market of people, LEB/S, who **you are and what you stand for and why you do what you do** are reliable parts of the new formula to winning the hearts and minds of your prospective clients, patients, and customers.

The under-appreciated advantage of doing this is creating a unilateral relationship with your clients, patients, and customers by telling the story of you, who you are, and what you stand for. Whether this is for a company, practice, or individual, this action often generates deep feelings of agreement and, occasionally, outright affection! Liking is a powerful stimulant in the marketplace; don't underestimate the power of this. Simply doing this when so many others will not gives you a powerful advantage.

In working with clients for my consulting services we go through an exercise to uncover these very principles, including a company's values, culture, and principles of who you are, how you think, and what you consider important. The breakthrough results show themselves in increased revenues and a powerful sense of ownership from all members of your practice or small business.

Refuse to Be Commoditized

What you offer to your market can be differentiated in many ways. Ideally, you are the only one who can provide the offering. This is true of patent medicines, patented systems, and protected intellectual property that can be obtained only through you and your company or practice.

Most professionals and small businesses are missing an opportunity to become the only or preferred source of their offering to LEB/S simply because they have assumed that differentiation can't be done.

The reality is that *virtually all offerings can be made different* in a way that matters to LEB/S. When you think of your offering as a commodity, you are virtually assured of being on the losing end of a continuing battle for profitable success. Why? Because commodities are bought based on the cheapest price for the products that are considered identical. If you have let your offerings fall into this trap, you have put yourself and those who buy from you at a severe disadvantage; you, because of the profit that rightfully should have been yours, and your buyer because of your handicapped ability to deliver anything but a plain vanilla product.

So what should your messaging to LEB/S do to differentiate you from every other perceived competitor? How do you make the competition irrelevant?

While many volumes have been written on this very subject, here is a useful list of seven differentiators to apply to your marketing and your team's mindset. (Note: Dozens more can be found by going to www.MasterYourPractice.com/differences for a free download.)

1. *Authorship—write a book.* This is the open secret that so many miss yet is used by the most famous of people. There is a reason that political candidates write books, why already famous people write books, and why those who aspire to being famous should write books.

   Books are part of our cultural DNA that says authors of books are experts, should be treated differently, and deserve our respect.

   At one time getting a book published was quite difficult. And with that difficulty, when overcome, came a special status of *author!* Authors are given respect and to some degree reverence in our society. It is this special status that makes authoring a book so powerful in your marketing. And it is one of the reasons I have written five and have another two coming. Moreover, writing a book conveys expert status and a bit of celebrity. Even if the book you get done is read only by your prospective clients, patients, or customers, a book (or books) can make you famous right where you live. Who else has written a book in your marketplace in your locale? Probably no one. And if there should be someone, what better way to fight fire with fire than getting your own book published? (I have a special co-authoring program for dentists should you be interested.)

2. *Public Speaking, like authorship, carries a cultural imprimatur of specialness.* Teaching does as well. If you speak or teach, you should let others know to increase others' respect for you as an individual and an expert in your field. Providing depth of content in articles and blogs and online presence also builds on your status as an authority.

Notice that these first two are about who you are.

3. *Resonant Communication.* Communication is the key to gaining attention and generating interest. <u>The error that most make is speaking in the vernacular of the knowing.</u> Your patients, clients, and customers don't know. The words they use to describe what they want and what attracts them are keys in grabbing their attention. Using the words they use that relate to your niche or area of expertise allows your messages to resonate in agreement with what they know. That permits attention to be gained in the first place! How do you find the words? Survey your users and prospects and use the results to craft your messages and further edit and curate your existing messages. The difference between the right and the wrong words is

like the difference between a lightning bug and a lightning bolt! (A paraphrase of Abraham Lincoln's words of wisdom.) The rule is: Know the words they use and use them to create effective marketing messages.

4. *Niche(s) where others aren't.* The great advantage of being in a niche where others are not is that you become impossible to compare. When you can get this, seize the moment to be the first, as the position will help you from here on out. Typically, others will follow you into the niche, jockeying for some of that success you have acquired by being the first one. There is a downside: You'll have to make the market, meaning you'll have to explain and market the concept of your offering first before you can market exactly what you do.

   A real coup is when you can go into an existing niche market and become dominant by employing the strength of your outward communication skills by being an author of a book, a speaker or teacher, as well as communicating in the easily understood words of your users.

5. *Sophistication and Diversity of Marketing.* Most want to simplify and reduce the various ways they can get their message across. Big mistake. Embrace diversity and complexity and sophistication because others will not want to follow and you'll have a built in advantage. Differentiation can come from marketing diversity itself.

6. *Celebrity—Becoming Slightly Famous Right Where You Live.* Becoming a celebrity right where you live is the result of your book, promotion, publicity, and public presence. Done well, celebrity enhances every part of your marketing, making it more memorable and effective. Moreover, few of your competitors understand the power of celebrity and its uses. For LEB/S, celebrity attracts their attention and makes your messages get through more easily.

7. *Doing What You Do So Well.* Being good at what you do and giving proof of your results in the forms of photos, statistics, awards, recognitions, certifications, testimonials, and endorsements from your clients, patients, or customers are in many ways the best marketing and promotion. Results are, after all, what people want from you. Promoting these results helps set you apart from the rest.

The more you can stack these and other differentiators one on top of the other, the more differentiation occurs. The better differentiated you are, the less price sensitivity you face and the more attractive you become to your targeted marketplace. Fees and prices become even more secondary.

Without giving a potential purchaser the "reasons why" that build value beyond commoditization, price does become the number-one issue. "After all, if the offerings are all alike, why shouldn't I buy based on the lowest price?" is the unspoken, subconscious mantra of the typical consumer.

This failure to differentiate "enough" is the common error that leads to commodity-based pricing. This means that you must continually separate your offerings from others. The greater the differentiation that matters to your ideal client, the greater power for profit in the marketplace as pricing and fees assume their rightful position in your customers' minds. What virtually every person wants is outstanding value. Differentiation builds that value.

Differentiation with Lead-Generation Marketing for LEB/S

Here is a competitive fact that gives you an advantage. If you market to gather leads of people who have some interest in your offering, you can pre-empt other marketing that competitors place. Most unsophisticated marketers do one-step marketing.

Ad placed, response to your practice or business or not. Over. Done. There is a better way.

Give people more than one way to respond, and ask for them to give you a "micro yes." Ask for a small decision, one they can easily make. Lead-generation marketing only asks for a "little yes." It asks who has some level of interest in what you offer. This interest can vary from "hot for what you got" to merely warm. By gathering the contact information of all those who express interest, you can be there with the "first-est" and "most-est" information.

Gathering leads allows you to spend more time, effort, and energy on those who self-select based on interest. Now you can afford to nurture, teach, and guide those who are interested in what you have. You can teach them how they should buy. This is a key point: 99.9% of your prospects do not know what to ask or what is important. YOU can and should provide this information as you nurture the prospective patient, client, or customer. When you do this, you are setting the buying criteria, a key advantage.

Moreover, now you can use offline and online media together to ensure that you are the presumptive choice. Your book, direct-mail letters, emails, audios, DVDs, web videos, and more become viable options and cost-effective ones. By teaching them how to think about and buy your offering, you become the sensible and logical choice when the time comes for decision.

Because most people considering a major decision can take months (and even years) of considering and cogitating before deciding on who will provide the service or product, lead generation gives you an advantage that most of your competitors skip over or ignore.

LEB/S *like* getting all this information and attention. They appreciate the efforts to help them. They may keep all the materials in a file for ready reference when decision time comes. Plus, they are likely to pass along your marketing materials to others who may have similar needs and wants. I have personally had patients come into my unique dental practice <u>years</u> after the initial response to my marketing.

What follows are examples of copyrighted lead-nurturing pieces sent in multiple mailings over time. Not shown are the emails and phone calls made to engage the prospective patient further.

FIGURE 16.1

FIGURE 16.2

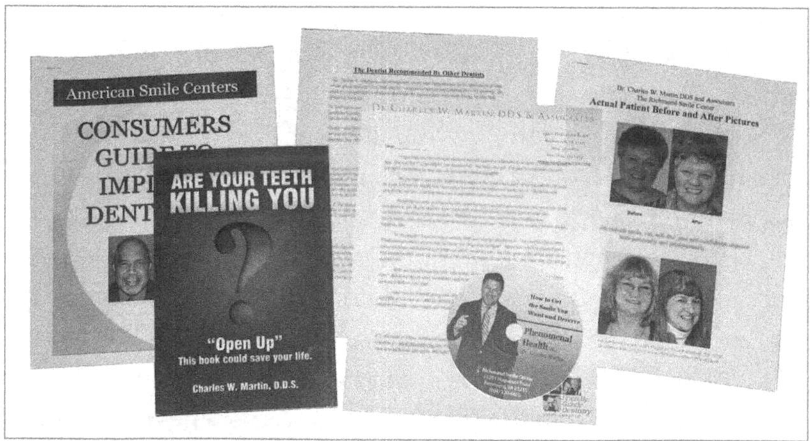

FIGURE 16.3

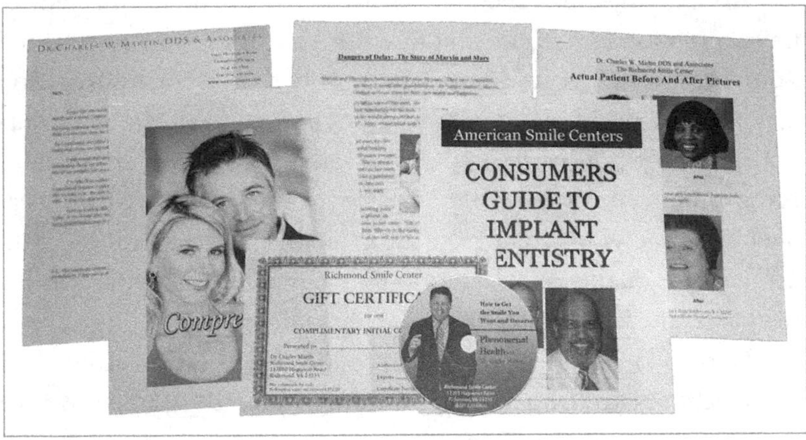

These examples show copyrighted materials sent to new patients. What is sent varies based on the request of new patients, the result of our dental health counselor's phone interview and other pieces already received.

Note the extensive use of books I have written for my target market. Figure 16.4 shows how we place sticky notes with a personal message on the outside cover.

FIGURE 16.4

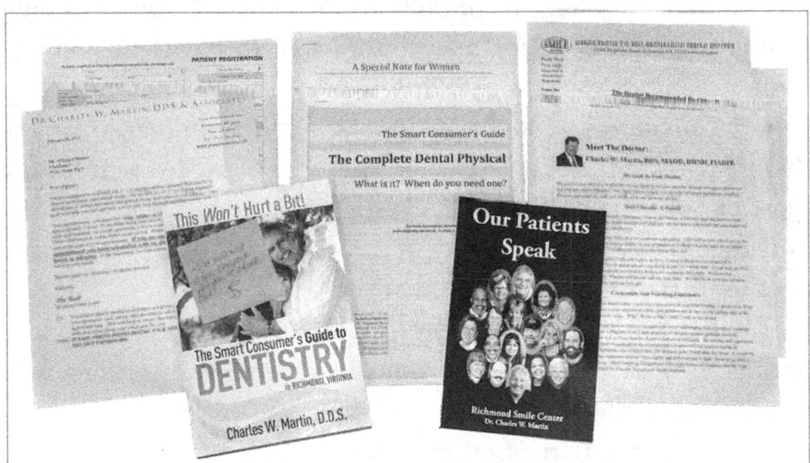

This can be done in the offline world and the online world.

An exciting new avenue has arisen from the online world. Once a person has an interest in what you offer, they most often go online to search for information. This search for information can be your decided advantage if you will use all the materials you have artfully compiled and created for offline efforts and bring them online. Moreover, online provides you with digital avenues that were heretofore unavailable or too expensive to implement in the offline world. This means that your online presence must be strong, thorough, and deep.

Here is key advice: Make a list of all the questions that your prospective clients/patients/customers ask in the course of making decisions. Now use one page per question to answer it on your website. This is prized content that your prospects want. Give it to them.

The new reality is that as the web continues to grow in importance and use, more and more LEB/S will use it like their younger counterparts to glean the information they need to make decisions.

Now, in many arenas of life and marketing, checking out the subject online before making a decision is a crucial part of the decision process for tens of millions of people. Its use will only grow. I have known for many years that this was happening. Now, many more affluent LEB/S pride themselves on being smart consumers who have done their due diligence online before making the first call to your practice or business. It is now part of your job as a wise marketer to be there when they are looking and provide guidance and help. This requires a website or sites that are robust, and full of content.

Whether driven online by a promotion or simply going online to search based on perceived needs or wants, your web presence must be significant and growing. The web has become a virtual town square of information and commerce.

FIGURE 16.5

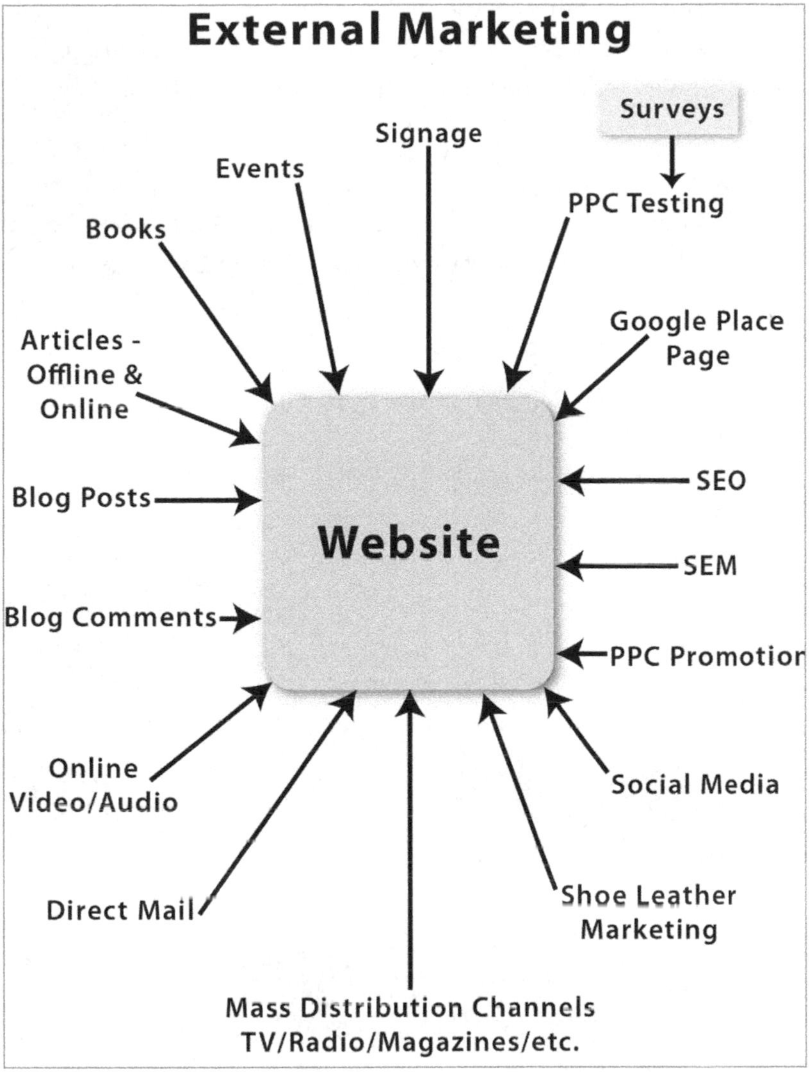

Social media is still in its relative infancy, and I expect that over time its use as marketing media will grow. Already a new term, "social commerce," has arisen to describe this. Some businesses have used social media as the primary method of growth, particularly for online businesses. But beware of over-dependence on online methods of marketing. It is noteworthy to recognize that the largest online players including Google also use offline ads and direct mail to promote themselves!

Dr. Martin works with professional practices and some small businesses and can be reached via his website at www.MasterYourPractice.com, or by phone at (866) 263-5577.

CHAPTER 17

The Power of "FOR ME"
Customization, Exclusivity, and Membership

Dan Kennedy

There is a famous story about a major city's streetcars, when doors had to be closed manually by the passengers—and weren't. Signs were posted, reading "As a Courtesy to All Passengers, Please Close the Doors." Ineffectual, they were replaced with "For Your Safety and Comfort, Please Close the Doors." I have had similar results with different wording, giving instructions to seminar attendees about returning from break and retaking seats on time, without loitering and requiring herding. FOR ME is very powerful.

When you are a senior, it is even more powerful because you feel you have earned special consideration by your years of toil, your accumulated wisdom, your elder statesman status. You also know you have special needs. You know that the same product, service, place, experience, or person that satisfies a wide swath of ages will likely not satisfy you.

When you are a boomer, FOR ME is also very powerful, for we are the FOR ME GENERATION. It's nearly DNA.

The Power of Customization

Customization is *the* desire. Harry Dent, Jr., wrote, back in 2004, of "the revolt of the affluent"—a rising resistance to off-the-shelf, one-size-fits-all, generic products, services, and experiences. I expanded on the theme in 2008, in the first edition of my book, *No B.S. Marketing to the Affluent*. In recent years, I've grown ever more strident in cautioning my clients that "tolerance for ordinary is over."

This is true for all LEB/S consumers, truest for affluent LEB/S, and truer now than it was a handful of years ago. Its edge is sharper. Its influence more powerful. The recession has reminded even the affluent of "value." It has reminded seniors of their parents' Great Depression lessons. For those not required to be frugal, it hasn't really prompted frugality so much as it has encouraged heightened sensitivity to and impatience with poor or even mediocre service, particularly if coupled with perceived disrespect; with less than exceptional experiences. It has made the LEB/S consumer more critical. My friend, Pete Lillo, a handful of years older than I, has grown more and more committed to his favorite motto: "You have to give me *a very good* reason to leave my house."

One of the problems in play here has to do with the pleasure of anticipation versus the pain of disappointment. Studies discussed on CBS's *Sunday Morning* program revealed that taking vacations rarely produces much happiness, and that afterward, people having had a vacation and those who have been home and at work the whole time register no discernible difference in objective psychological measurements of expressed happiness. In fact, most vacation returnees tell their friends and co-workers of the disappointments of the trips, and may also be more irritable and unhappy for days or weeks after their return. Happiness is produced before the trip, from the anticipation of the vacation. People instinctively know this about themselves. The other study mentioned on the TV program had to do with the offer of a kiss from a celebrity of one's choice. You and most people, have, at different times, held crushes on celebrities. When offered actual romantic connection with their crush, and given the choice of the little tryst occurring that very day, the next day, two days hence, or three days hence, people chose three days away by a big majority. Immediate fulfillment would rob them of all the anticipation.

Younger consumers have a more resilient response to the disappointment that so often trails great, positive anticipation. Hopes for a great night out fulfilled with only an ordinary night, or even a profoundly disappointing night, are easily shrugged off—after all, it's just one night, life is long. A problem-riddled vacation that falls far short of its anticipation, well, there are a lot of vacations to come. Money spent on a much anticipated trip, evening out, gift for a family member, or product for the home that proves disappointing, well, there will be a lot more money made and, heck, in 10, 20 years, it will be irrelevant. Not so for us LEB/S. We are, as the saying goes, on or approaching the back 9, and we can see the clubhouse in the distance; we're not teeing off toward the first hole. That *is* a LEB/S saying. We are quite aware of where we are. The number of "next" vacations, next home remodeling projects, next investments, next times we place trust in some advisor, even next nights out is finite. Every night I climb into the racing sulky, take the reins of a racehorse, and head out to the parade to the post, I say to myself, "There will be a last time for this."

Penn, of Penn & Teller, was born in 1955. He is a LE-boomer. His father was a prison guard and, on the side, a numismatic dealer in coins. His parents bought him an Amazing Kreskin magic kit as a birthday present, at a young age, and thereby stamped an ambition that would guide his life. He went through the Barnum & Bailey and Ringling Brothers Clown College. He once performed an act involving riding a unicycle while juggling toilet plungers. (Note: not knives.) Penn developed what he calls "the first rule of show business" early: Never take a restaurant job. A bad day in show business is better than a good day of dishwashing. He worked as an itinerant street performer. He fought his way onto *The Howard Stern Show.* About his (and Teller's) enormously popular, long-running Las Vegas show, I have witnessed him saying and writing, more than once, "There will be a last time for this."

If you are a LEB/S, doing something you like, you know there will be a last time for this.

For this reason, LEB/S consumers grow ever more frustrated by the cycle of hopeful anticipation and sad disappointment. We are conscious of it. We are cautious in our anticipation and keenly interested in avoiding the pain of disappointment. Customization fuels hopeful anticipation, because it promises to prevent disappointment. When you are very clearly positioned and presented as a "specialist" in your category of goods or services, for the LEB/S, you trigger positive anticipation thanks to the "Oh, that's FOR ME" factor. This is what the words "*relaxed fit* jeans" mean to a LEB/S with fluctuating weight or a spare tire around his waist. This is what a "*calm and peaceful* oceanfront resort" means to a LEB/S worried about being surrounded by party animals or families with screaming children. This is what "dedicated to *preserving* clients' *hard-earned life savings* with *personalized* guaranteed-income investment plans" means to the LEB/S considering financial advisors.

But, should you then deliver disappointing experiences, you'll get no second chances. Back in 2004, Dent wrote that "the revolution is about real-time, personalized service at lower costs to meet the needs of a rapidly expanding affluent consumer who expects and demands such service, and creating an ongoing service revenue (relationship) versus a one-time product sale." If you substitute LEB/S consumer in place of the generic affluent consumer in this statement, you have a solid prescription for the best approach to the LEB/S market.

The Power of Exclusivity

Del Webb, the leading developer of retirement communities, has to deal with this issue of age restriction; whether to require residents be of a certain age. This has been a fact of life in the retirement community industry for quite some time, but has oddly not migrated to most other industries. I could definitely see select airline flights to places like Orlando and Las Vegas being designated for LEB/S or seniors only, with planes equipped to more easily accommodate these passengers, and with families traveling with small children precluded. I once suggested Disney setting aside a concierge floor and lounge in its resort hotels exclusively for adults there without children, to create a quieter, less chaotic setting. The Imagineers I had the discussion with thought it antithetical to Disney culture, but didn't summarily reject it—especially given my suggestion that guests might pay as much as a 50% premium for the exclusivity. This hasn't happened, although Disney is a big exclusivity marketer in many ways, notably including extra-priced, variable-priced Fast Pass, VIP Private Guides (Human Fast Passes right to the front of every line), Concierge Floors, and activities only available to those guests, such as the behind-scenes dawn safari at Animal Kingdom, etc.

The question is: How many LEB/S *want* exclusivity by segregation?

The "2010 Del Webb's Boomer Survey" revealed that trailing-edge boomers are ambivalent about age-restricted communities, with about 10% more interest among LE-boomers. Within their own clientele of Del Webb residents planning to make a second move as retirees, the preference for age-restricted communities leaps sky high, to 10–1. This reveals that the exclusivity preference rises with age, but it also reveals it is dramatically affected *by experience*. It is my own pet theory that LEB/S consumers and particularly senior consumers will have greater preference for age-based exclusivity in just about any business category after having experienced it. In that regard, it may be less useful as an attractant of new clients than as a retention/loyalty strategy with continuing customers.

Exclusivity plays a very big role in marketing to the affluent, which I deal with in depth in the *No B.S. Guide to Marketing to the Affluent*. Exclusivity can also enhance trust, as discussed in *No B.S. Trust-Based Marketing*.

I now travel distances only by private jet. I've been on only one commercial flight—overseas—in the past three years. It is my most outrageous indulgence, although to be fair, the value of my time when invested in my work tops $2,000.00 an hour, and most of my work requires a great deal of focus and mental concentration, so saving a half day, day, or days of time tied to a trip can be worth as much as or more than the cost of the private jet, and arriving at the destination or back home to work in a good frame of mind has monetary value. Still, my best defense aside, it's indulgent. I've paid a lot of attention, the five years or so I've been traveling this way, to my own thoughts about it and to my observations of and conversations with others in the private terminals we embark and arrive at. It's my sense that it is only a minority of these travelers who are glitz-and-glitter celebrities, the famous rich, feeding ego, or even markedly elitist; most of them have more in common with me. Their motives are not so much the luxury of this mode of travel as escape from the profound unpleasantness and inconvenience of the ordinary alternative. Their relationship with the exclusivity of private jets is not so much status as it is segregation.

Most major hospitals now quietly segregate. They have "secret" and not-so-secret suites and even entire floors reserved only for the rich and famous, the rich and powerful, and the quiet rich, including their own chief donors. The area where the "executive physicals" are conducted is set apart from the area that most patients visit staff doctors for routine physicals. Since there is marked convergence with affluence and LEB/S status, most of these privileged patients are LEB/S, and they welcome, even if they didn't at first seek, this exclusivity, as much or more for the segregation as for any special benefits.

In marketing to LEB/S, we're making the point often throughout this book that you need your business, products, services, and messaging to be for LEB/S, and to be clearly for LEB/S. I go farther with my advocacy of exclusivity. I believe you also need to be quite clear about who you *aren't* for. Cadillac and Lincoln have, I think wisely, done this in most of their advertising in 2011 and 2012, depicting, at youngest, boomers and more often LEB/S, and using language crafted to call out to LEB/S and exclude younger consumers. It seems to be paying dividends. Were I creating the advertising, I would likely be less subtle.

In its extensive research study of 2010, "Approaching 65: A Survey of Baby Boomers Turning 65 Years Old," AARP noted that "there is a sense among members of the baby boom population that they are special or unique." We LEB/S were raised to believe just that. It is deeply ingrained, and to me, all the more reason to play the age-linked exclusivity card in every way possible.

The Power of Membership

The behemoth of the LEB/S marketplace is AARP.

If you haven't received your first of a very persistent series of mailings complete with your already personalized membership card, I have bad news for you: You most certainly will. You will not be permitted to ignore this pronouncement from on high that YOU ARE OLD!, as you might skip town on your birthday, avoid dinner invites or surprise parties, leave cards unopened. You can't lie or joke about your number either. AARP *knows*.

Few of its 40,000,000 members know of its origins, true purpose or power, not necessarily wielded in members' best interests. But the majority of LEB/S consumers are influenced by its endorsement for commercial products and services, and their lives are influenced by its lobbying, like it or not.

AARP is the world's second largest nonprofit organization, after the Catholic Church. Both wear the nonprofit mantle yet own and operate a number of richly profitable businesses and investments. While the Catholic Church confines itself more to passive investments than active business invention and operation, AARP is the opposite. It began as a scheme to sell insurance. It is, itself, a boomer. In 1958, a then-72-year-old retired high school principal, Ethel Andrus, was frustrated that she and others like her could not obtain health insurance at fair rates because of age, and had the idea of banding together such individuals to negotiate as a group with the insurance industry. Her noble idea was altered to a money-making opportunity by a 32-year-old, ambitious and opportunistic insurance broker, Leonard Davis, who offered to help her in her cause, for a price. He provided $50,000.00 in seed capital and expert advice to launch her organization, initially for retired schoolteachers (not just any old persons). In exchange, he secured the exclusive rights to sell not only health, but also life insurance and other financial products to its members. Permanently. In its infancy, Davis brokered the insurance, but when the organization was morphing into AARP and topping 750,000 members, he formed his own insurance company. You may have heard of it. Colonial Penn. By the early 1970s, Davis was selling insurance to 10 million AARP members. His net profits exceeded $200 million.

That's gumball machine money compared to today's AARP. It is still an insurance sales juggernaut, generating hundreds of millions of dollars of commissions to AARP from a consortium of auto, home, health, disability, life, travel, and burial insurers, plus commissions from approved and endorsed providers of a dizzying array of other LEB/S-oriented products and services, sponsorship fees from giant pharma, bank, credit card, travel, and other corporate partners, and one of the highest per-page ad rates of any print magazine for its publications, the flagship of which is *Modern Maturity.* Exclusivity is often sold, presumably to the highest bidder. Lockout from the captive and controlled audience of LEB/S consumers swayed by AARP recommendation is used as a bloody axe in negotiations. I have witnessed it all firsthand with a client of mine involved with senior health care.

AARP brilliantly melds the power of membership, the patina of an objective advocacy organization, its nonprofit status, and its charitable activities to secure high trust from its members (customers) and create unrivaled value for its advertisers, sponsors, exclusive vendors, and other business partners. It has built a large, powerful "toll booth," virtually uncontested by competitors, and it collects very stiff tolls from any and every marketer seeking to pass through the gates. It may well be *the* ultimate example of what I teach as business and marketing strategy: ownership of the toll position. (A concept I first learned in the 1970s from a brilliant entrepreneur, Harvey Brody, to give credit where credit is due.)

If the AARP were a for-profit corporation, it might very well have run afoul of federal anti-trust laws by now, but its shield of nonprofit status is strong. It is made even stronger by AARP's lobbying arm. It employs dozens of staff lobbyists along with outside PR firms, other Washington lobbyists, and ex-congressmen as "advisors"; essentially a small militia of influencers. It is also able to mobilize its giant army of members in letter-writing, email, and telephone campaigns directed at elected officials and the media. That army, incidentally, dwarfs the membership of the National Rifle Association, the Boy Scouts of America, the National PTA, and the AFL-CIO, combined. When told that both Ronald Reagan and George Bush had "dissed" the AARP by neglecting to involve its representatives in White House-level discussions about health care and other senior issues, President Clinton asked, "Couldn't they count?" Meaning, couldn't the presidents count *votes*? Or *money?*

The AARP also pours millions into "issue advertising" on TV, radio, and in print, to directly influence elections as well as to push or oppose legislation. (There was a view during Hillary's push for universal health care that AARP was opposing it in every way possible, openly and behind closed doors, more because of its own financial interests as an insurance marketer than for any benefit of its members. Its position on so-called "Obamacare" has been more nuanced, but is nonetheless suspected by many.) AARP also funds research on anti-aging, giant conferences in pleasant resorts, and serves as a "source" for the same media that might be critical of it. It is, in effect, a giant octopus, with tentacles reaching to every politician's pocket at every level of government, into every media outlet, and into every area of commercial enterprise touching LEB/S. I have even drawn data from and quoted its research elsewhere in this book—research prepared primarily for use by its commercial partners with purpose common to this book's; guiding them in more effectively selling more goods and services to these consumers.

It can't go without mention that AARP has a major financial advantage over any commercial, capitalist competitors: As a nonprofit institution, it pays no income taxes. However, the strategic principles underpinning its power and success can be co-opted by any business, even at the small local level. They are:

1. Membership
2. Mission Larger Than Itself & Its Own Interests
3. Toll Position
4. Influence

Membership has power because all seniors and many LE-boomers are preconditioned to want it and value it. Seniors have been joiners and belongers their entire lives. All the fraternal organizations, like Kiwanis, Rotary, Elks, etc., have been most actively supported by "The Greatest Generation." Even Fred Flintstone and Barney Rubble belonged to a lodge. Bowling leagues, now in decline, thrived in my parents' day. Joining, belonging to, being identified with and, in many cases, advancing in groups was a path to status for these consumers, in youth and all through adult life.

If you examine the "control" direct-mail pieces of a great many entities marketing themselves to LEB/S, to recruit customers, subscribers, or donors, you will find the already personalized membership card affixed to the sales letter, showing through a window in the envelope, and you will find membership language used throughout. The week I was finishing this chapter, I received a very elaborate mailing of this kind from the Sierra Club. These cards add cost to these mailings, and when hundreds of thousands or even millions of pieces are being mailed, every added cost matters. Most of these major mailers conduct extensive split tests, pitting different offers, mailing formats, colors, and other variables against each other, and it's a very safe wager they've tested membership card vs. no membership card. You can assume the use of the card bumps response more than enough to justify the cost. I'm not necessarily making the micro-suggestion you create membership cards for your coffee shop or beauty parlor (although I wouldn't necessarily rule it out). I call this membership card tactic to your attention as illustration of the broader point: The membership *concept* is powerful with LEB/S.

If you look into GKIC, beginning with the offer on page 264, you will discern that, like AARP, we are a money-making operation, in our case publishing newsletters and online training, hosting conferences, providing various exclusive resources and services, and serving as a portal for approved and endorsed vendors, to a "membership association" of marketing-minded entrepreneurs, small-business owners, self-employed and private practice professionals, and sales professionals in the U.S. and in about a dozen other countries. We have local chapters meeting regularly in nearly a hundred cities. We have a ladder of ascension for members to move from one membership level to another. We have achievement awards. We are, in effect, a service organization to our members, and a marketing machine for our own goods as well as for a consortium of vendor-partners, sponsors, and advertisers. Our sister, the Information Marketing Association (www.info-marketing.org), is a smaller clone of GKIC, for authors and thought leaders, niche industry consultants and advisors, business and life coaches, publishers, and seminar, workshop, and conference impresarios. The AARP model was not lost on me. I started it all with four subscribers, a newsletter made on a photocopy machine. It now has private equity investment and professional management, a staff exceeding 50, and some 25,000 members, but, beyond that, over 350,000 online, opt-in subscribers and catalog customers, a network of grassroots independent business consultants, a global network of nice industry consultants, and thus a yearly reach of more than one million business owners. Although GKIC members encompass the entire adult age range, the majority of our higher-level members are LEB/S.

Mission larger than self is also influential with LEB/S. After all, seniors sacrificed to save the world and boomers set out from the very start to change the world. Even the small, local business can involve itself in charitable activities of interest to LEB/S residents of its city or community. Organizations like the Arthritis Foundation are nationwide in scope, but have local chapters, local events, and local segments of their national telethon. If you are going to reposition your business as a membership entity, know that LEB/S like belonging, but they are even prouder of belonging to something that is doing good.

Toll position applies at all levels. Often, the best small-ball use of toll position is in co-operative marketing and list and endorsement exchange with another marketer(s) who also owns toll booths to LEB/S customers you desire. The implant dentist and the Lasik® doctor can co-operate and can exchange. The financial advisor and the estate lawyer can co-operate and exchange. But don't neglect opportunities to extract cash tolls for the access you offer or the customers you can deliver. If you can bring 50 affluent LEB/S "members" to a winery on a "member appreciation outing," you shouldn't be paying the winery; they should be paying you. And if one is too obtuse to recognize the opportunity, someone can be made to see it.

Influence. People love those who speak for them. Rush Limbaugh's popularity and wealth is derived from his articulation of philosophies and viewpoints his listeners already have, on their behalf, through his microphone—a microphone they do not have. Any local business owner can make himself into a vocal advocate for groups and causes. At bare minimum, he can "stand for" his LEB/S customers and their values and views via pronouncements in his own media—customer newsletters, blogs, and such. He can write and have published a "viewpoint book" that he gifts to his clients, and through his clients, to his friends. You can go further. You can give national voice to your views, in much the same way I do, by writing articles, by writing books, by promoting yourself to the media. It isn't nearly as difficult as you might think, because the media is now 24 hours a day, 7 days a week, huge, with an insatiable appetite for new faces, strong viewpoints, and interesting human interest stories. One tip about relating to the LEB/S consumer that I consistently give to financial advisors, lawyers, doctors, and others I coach is: They want to know who you are and what you think and believe, not just what you sell.

CHAPTER 18

The Power of Special Occasion Marketing

Dean Killingbeck

Over the last nine years I have helped over 32 different types of businesses develop and implement event and holiday marketing systems, including financial planning, dentistry, chiropractic, restaurants, auto repair, and more. During those nine years, I've found that all businesses have two things in common: They all need more new customers, and they all need additional cash flow. However, both objectives don't necessarily go hand-in-hand. In fact, the cost of acquiring a new customer many times outweighs the profitability of that new customer's ROI (return on investment), creating a negative cash flow. Consequently, that's why my company has created over 113 different direct-marketing pieces for event and holiday marketing that can be brutally and honestly measured to make sure that our clients receive a positive ROI.

It's Easy to Invite LEB/S Consumers to Events

If there's one thing we know for sure about LEB/S, it's that they still read and open up their mail, and they enjoy it! If you don't believe me, ask a few of them if they would rather receive a handwritten thank-you note or one by email. Also, my clients have realized that LEB/S are the most loyal customers because they don't necessarily take their business someplace else to save $0.05, $0.10, or $10.00. They will remain loyal to the business that shows them respect, keeps their word, and says "Thank You." Let me repeat myself: Most of the time, LEB/S like to receive a mailed "Thank You" note. They are not looking for the next tweet, text, or new app.

Special Occasion Marketing 101

I need to give you a quick background about Special Occasion Marketing via direct mail. Event marketing uses two very successful marketing strategies: 1) a story; and 2) a list.

Every special occasion marketing campaign must have a story. When you use stories to tell customers why you're offering them something special, it makes your "event" credible and you become believable. This is especially true for LEB/S. Most seniors were even raised before the age of TV and were brought up listening to the radio for entertainment. Being 67 years old myself, I can remember well how my mother, dad, sister, and I sat around the radio listening to stories (my favorite was *The Lone Ranger*). I also remember sitting outside with my grandfather on an 80° summer night, him in his rocker and me on the ground pounding my mitt, listening to a Detroit Tigers' baseball game, booing the bad calls and each high and wide pitch. Back then, it truly was all about the "story." I read in a marketing book somewhere that "stories sell, facts just tell" and I've believed in that strategy throughout my marketing career.

The second strategy in successful Special Occasion Marketing is using a proper list. As with any good marketing campaign, it truly is all about the list! With the advances in data management and the amount of information list brokers can narrow down, we can now target very specific demographics. Age, household income, geographical location (as specific as carrier routes), birth month, whether or not they're married, veterans in the household, children in the household, etc., all have an impact on how successful your campaign will be.

Let me give you an example of good list segmentation: David A. from the Washington, DC, area owns a high-end film company and was getting ready for a new direct-mail campaign. Instead of a generic list of high-net-worth individuals in the area, he wanted to target only those high-net-worth individuals who were celebrating milestone birthdays in the upcoming months. Now, normally, I think of milestone birthdays as the ages of 40, 50, or 60. However, in his company's case, the birthday milestones that he wanted to specifically target were the ages of 75, 80, 85, and 90. David's company had found out through the years that the older generation, 75 and older, was more interested in preserving memories than the younger generations. So the demographics we used were: homeowners with a household income of $250,000.00 or more, a home value over $1 million, living within the Washington, DC, metro area.

We found a total of 1,001 people celebrating their specific milestone birthday so that his company could approach them with a great story of how they can pass down a film legacy to their grandchildren and great-grandchildren.

Use Holiday and Special Occasion Marketing as Your Personal ATM

Let's talk about how you can directly affect your business by selecting the "right" LEB/S that will fill your store, book of business, or service business by using specific event and holiday marketing.

Birthdays: The Number-One Best Marketing Occasion

The number-one best marketing event of the year is birthdays. Why? Because EVERYONE has a birthday and celebrates that birthday in some form, so this "event" relates to everyone! If you have the birthdays of your existing customers, mail them a birthday card or letter and offer them a FREE birthday gift. You can use birthdays to entice new customers to take action by giving them some type of an irresistible offer in the form of a birthday gift. We call this strategy "Cold Birthdays," where you send an offer to someone you've had no previous contact with. Yes, you can choose specific demographics AND find out their birthday year and month. On the next pages are a couple examples of our very successful mailers.

In Figure 18.1, Dusty's Cellar is using birthdays as a new customer acquisition system. How is it working? The numbers speak for themselves. He is very specific in who he targets for his mailers: LEB/S homeowners, with a household income of $100,000.00 or more who live within a three-mile radius of his restaurant. In Figure 18.1, you should notice three major statistics in his metrics that are consistent from month to month: First, because of this program, they have over 150 new customers visiting them each month for a total of at least 1,800 new guests per year. And, these aren't just any run-of-the-mill customers; they fit the LEB/S demographics that mirror Dusty's best customers. The second statistic is the percentage of redeemed gift certificates each month, which averages 25.8%—phenomenal results for a direct mail campaign to a "cold" list. The last statistic, which is the most important, is that Dusty's spends only $519.00 each month for these mailers, which generate an average cash flow of over $5,500.00 each month, receiving a 10 to 1 ROI!

FIGURE 18.1: Special-Occasion Marketing Piece Example

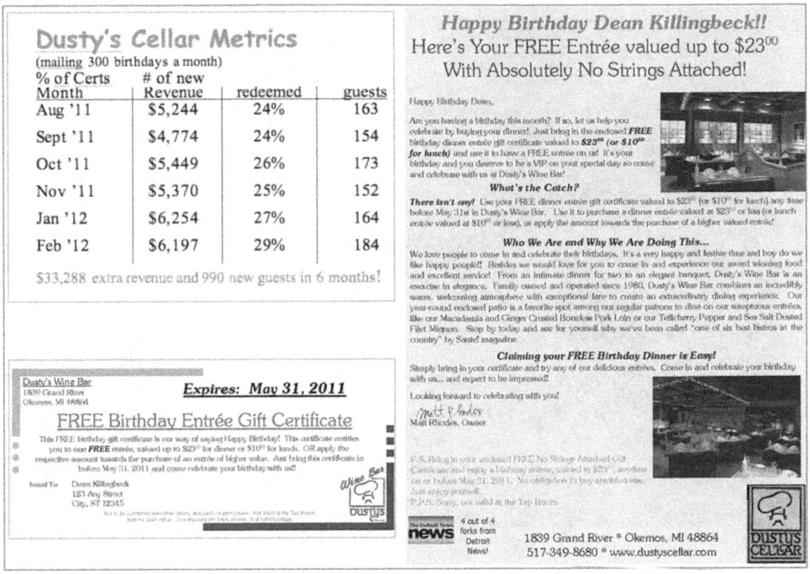

Dusty's Cellar Metrics
(mailing 300 birthdays a month)

% of Certs	# of new		
Month	Revenue	redeemed	guests
Aug '11	$5,244	24%	163
Sept '11	$4,774	24%	154
Oct '11	$5,449	26%	173
Nov '11	$5,370	25%	152
Jan '12	$6,254	27%	164
Feb '12	$6,197	29%	184

$33,288 extra revenue and 990 new guests in 6 months!

Dusty's Wine Bar
1839 Grand River
Okemos, MI 48864

Expires: May 31, 2011

FREE Birthday Entrée Gift Certificate

This FREE birthday gift certificate is our way of saying Happy Birthday! This certificate entitles you to one **FREE** entrée, valued up to 23^{00} for dinner or 10^{00} for lunch. OR apply the respective amount towards the purchase of an entrée of higher value. Just bring this certificate in before May 31, 2011 and come celebrate your birthday with us!

Issued To: Dean Killingbeck
123 Any Street
City, ST 12345

Wine Bar
Dusty's

Happy Birthday Dean Killingbeck!!
Here's Your FREE Entrée valued up to 23^{00}
With Absolutely No Strings Attached!

Happy Birthday Dean,

Are you having a birthday this month? If so, let us help you celebrate by buying your dinner! Just bring in the enclosed ***FREE*** birthday dinner entrée gift certificate valued to ***23^{00} (or 10^{00} for lunch)*** and use it to have a FREE entrée on us! It's your birthday and you deserve to be a VIP on your special day so come and celebrate with us at Dusty's Wine Bar!

What's the Catch?

There isn't any! Use your FREE dinner entrée gift certificate valued to 23^{00} (or 10^{00} for lunch) any time before May 31st in Dusty's Wine Bar. Use it to purchase a dinner entrée valued at 23^{00} or less (or lunch entrée valued at 10^{00} or less), or apply the amount towards the purchase of a higher valued entrée!

Who We Are and Why We Are Doing This...

We love people to come in and celebrate their birthdays. It's a very happy and festive time and boy do we like happy people!! Besides we would love for you to come in and experience our award winning food and excellent service! From an intimate dinner for two to an elegant banquet, Dusty's Wine Bar is an exercise in elegance. Family owned and operated since 1980, Dusty's Wine Bar combines an incredibly warm, welcoming atmosphere with exceptional fare to create an extraordinary dining experience. Our year-round enclosed patio is a favorite spot among our regular patrons to dine on our sumptuous entrées, like our Macadamia and Ginger Crusted Boneless Pork Loin or our Tellicherry Pepper and Sea Salt Dusted Filet Mignon. Stop by today and see for yourself why we've been called "one of six best bistros in the country" by Santé! magazine.

Claiming your FREE Birthday Dinner is Easy!

Simply bring in your certificate and try any of our delicious entrées. Come in and celebrate your birthday with us... and expect to be impressed!

Looking forward to celebrating with you!

Matt Rhodes
Matt Rhodes, Owner

P.S. Bring in your enclosed FREE No Strings Attached Gift Certificate and enjoy a birthday entrée, valued to 23^{00}, anytime on or before May 31, 2011. No obligation to buy anything else. Just enjoy yourself.
P.P.S. Sorry, not valid at the Tap Room.

The Detroit News news 4 out of 4 forks from Detroit News!

1839 Grand River * Okemos, MI 48864
517-349-8680 * www.dustyscellar.com

DUSTY'S CELLAR

But My Business Is Different!!!

I'm sure you're thinking, "But Dean. . . my business is different! Those birthday mailers will never work for me! Everyone celebrates their birthday at a restaurant, but it doesn't fit my business model!" Well, my friend, you're mistaken!

Let's take a look at another model where a client of mine uses birthdays. Bob Carr of TLC Garage Works, located in Gambrills, Maryland, who does garage makeovers by adding shelves and cupboards, uses birthdays as an opportunity to thank his current customers. Bob mails approximately 300 birthday cards every month to his house list and thanks them for their business (see Figure 18.2). He uses a greeting card with a picture of his own dog (Mighty Moe) on the front. Note: Dogs, kids, and humor draw attention to direct-mail pieces. Bob also inserts either a FREE pizza certificate or a Dunkin' Donuts gift card, and his customers LOVE him for it. Heck, I give my insurance agent thousands of

FIGURE 18.2: Personalized Birthday Thank-You Note Example

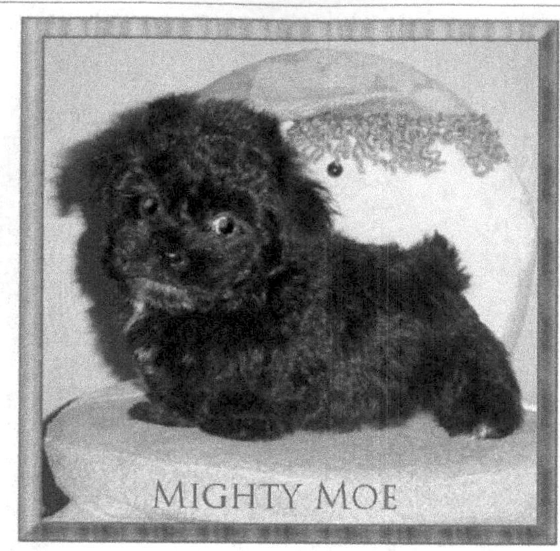

Happy Birthday John! From Mighty Moe and TLC!

dollars of business and don't even get an annual thank-you note! OK, I'll confess, if I walk into his office, he'll offer me a desk calendar and a pen, but it's just not the same. Remember, I'm 67 years old and expect a little more. A birthday card once a year telling me "thanks" would go a long way, considering that if an aggressive insurance salesperson approached me with the right attitude and a good story for switching, I would probably switch.

Check Mailers

Real Check Mailer–One of my favorite marketing pieces is a real check mailer that you can use to encourage sales from your existing clients, or as a new-client acquisition piece. The business sends a real check through the mail—yes, that's right, a REAL check. It is accompanied by a letter explaining why they are sending the check and offering an amazing discount 10 times the amount shown on the check (or whatever discount our clients want to do).

FIGURE 18.3: Check-Mailer Marketing Campaign Example

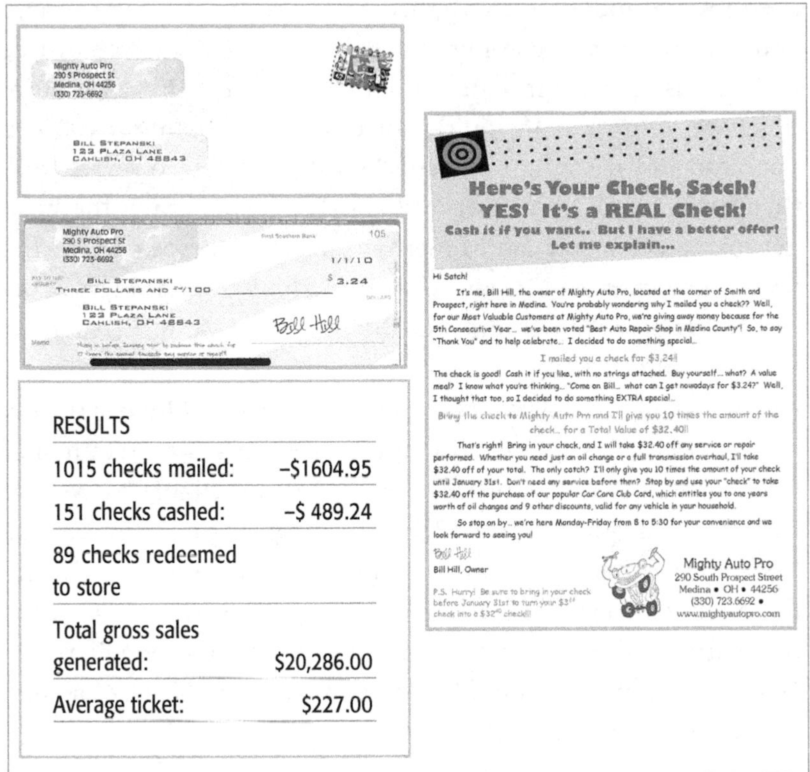

Mighty Auto Pro
290 S Prospect St
Medina, OH 44256
(330) 723-6692

BILL STEPANSKI
123 PLAZA LANE
CAHLISH, OH 48843

Mighty Auto Pro
290 S Prospect St
Medina, OH 44256
(330) 723-6692

First Southern Bank 105

1/1/10

BILL STEPANSKI $ 3.24
THREE DOLLARS AND 24/100

BILL STEPANSKI
123 PLAZA LANE
CAHLISH, OH 48843

Bill Hill

Memo

RESULTS	
1015 checks mailed:	-$1604.95
151 checks cashed:	-$ 489.24
89 checks redeemed to store	
Total gross sales generated:	$20,286.00
Average ticket:	$227.00

Here's Your Check, Satch!
YES! It's a REAL Check!
Cash it if you want.. But I have a better offer! Let me explain...

Hi Satch!

It's me, Bill Hill, the owner of Mighty Auto Pro, located at the corner of Smith and Prospect, right here in Medina. You're probably wondering why I mailed you a check?? Well, for our *Most Valuable Customers* at Mighty Auto Pro, we're giving away money because for the 5th *Consecutive Year*... we've been voted "Best Auto Repair Shop in Medina County"! So, to say "Thank You" and to help celebrate... I decided to do something special...

I mailed you a check for $3.24!

The check is good! Cash it if you like, with no strings attached. Buy yourself... what? A value meal? I know what you're thinking... "Come on Bill... what can I get nowadays for $3.24?" Well, I thought that too, so I decided to do something EXTRA special...

Bring the check to Mighty Auto Pro and I'll give you 10 times the amount of the check... for a Total Value of $32.40!!

That's right! Bring in your check, and I will take $32.40 off any service or repair performed. Whether you need just an oil change or a full transmission overhaul, I'll take $32.40 off of your total. The only catch? I'll only give you 10 times the amount of your check until January 31st. Don't need any service before then? Stop by and use your "check" to take $32.40 off the purchase of our popular *Car Care Club Card*, which entitles you to one years worth of oil changes and 9 other discounts, valid for any vehicle in your household.

So stop on by... we're here Monday-Friday from 8 to 5:30 for your convenience and we look forward to seeing you!

Bill Hill
Bill Hill, Owner

P.S. Hurry! Be sure to bring in your check before January 31st to turn your $3.24 check into a $32.40 check!!

Mighty Auto Pro
290 South Prospect Street
Medina • OH • 44256
(330) 723.6692 •
www.mightyautopro.com

We've used this mailer to celebrate an anniversary of a business, a wedding anniversary of a business owner, and Figure 18.3 is an example of how we used the mailer to celebrate the fifth year in a row that Bill and Leigh Anne from Mighty Auto Pro received the "Best Auto Repair Shop in Medina County" award.

They spent around $2,000.00 in order to achieve $20,000.00 in sales! That's a whopping 10 to 1 ROI! Also, the result that doesn't show up in the number crunching is that this was sent in January, during the worst recession in decades, and people were desperate for any cash they could get their hands on.

The folks that cashed the check truly needed it, and they have been forever indebted to Mighty Auto Pro for their generosity and are still great customers to this day! Also, as stated, this mailer was sent out in January. January in Ohio, in case you're unaware, is brutal! If you're not outside shoveling a path to your car and freezing your cheeks off in sub-zero wind chill, then basically all you want to do is stay home, crank the heat, get under a blanket, and hibernate. Except, of course, for the brave customers of Mighty Auto Pro who were willing to take on the terrible weather and take Bill and Leigh Anne up on their fantastic offer.

Tax Rebate Check–The other check mailer that I love is the tax rebate check mailer shown in Figure 18.4. This is a great mailer that can be used to spur sales from existing clients as well as be used to acquire new customers. Since it greatly resembles a tax return from the government, it works wonders during the months of February, March, and April. However, with the popularity of the government stimulus checks, these mailers can be used anytime throughout the year as an extra "slack adjuster" during your slow months.

Cause-Oriented Occasion Marketing

Using a cause for an event marketing strategy not only makes you money but also makes you feel good. One of the more popular

FIGURE 18.4: Tax Rebate Check Mailer Example

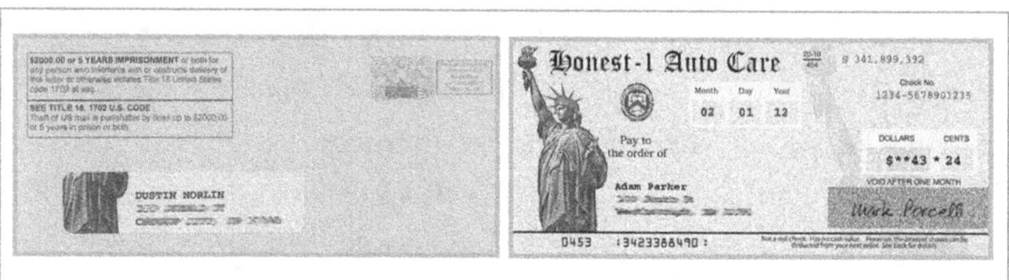

FIGURE 18.5: Cause-Oriented Marketing Example

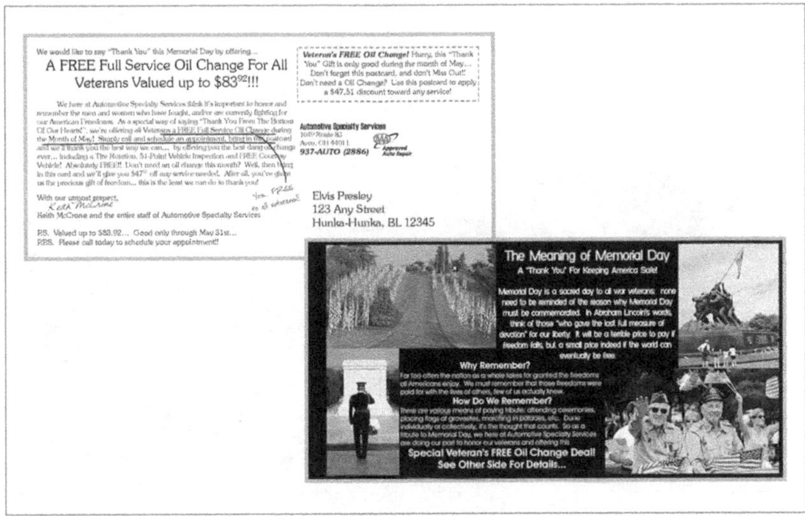

causes our clients use is a Memorial Day postcard giving free offers to veterans shown in Figure 18.5. We have heard stories of Vietnam vets coming in near tears (or even crying) because no one has ever given them anything for fighting for our country. Now let me tell you, that's truly gut-wrenching and sad, but ask Keith McCrone of Automotive Specialty Services if he felt proud to give a free oil change to that vet!

According to *Self* magazine, top causes that women feel strongly about are medical research to cure disease and child welfare. Our postcards for Breast Cancer Awareness and Toys for Tots fit both those causes (see Figure 18.6). The month of October is breast cancer awareness month, and I'm sure you've noticed that even the NFL promotes and contributes to the cause. Toys for Tots hits chords in both men and women, as well as veterans. Andy Nelson, owner of Andy Nelson's BBQ from Cockeysville, Maryland, offered a free dessert and a $1.00 contribution to Toys for Tots to anyone who brought in their postcard to his restaurant.

FIGURE 18.6: Direct-Mail Marketing Example

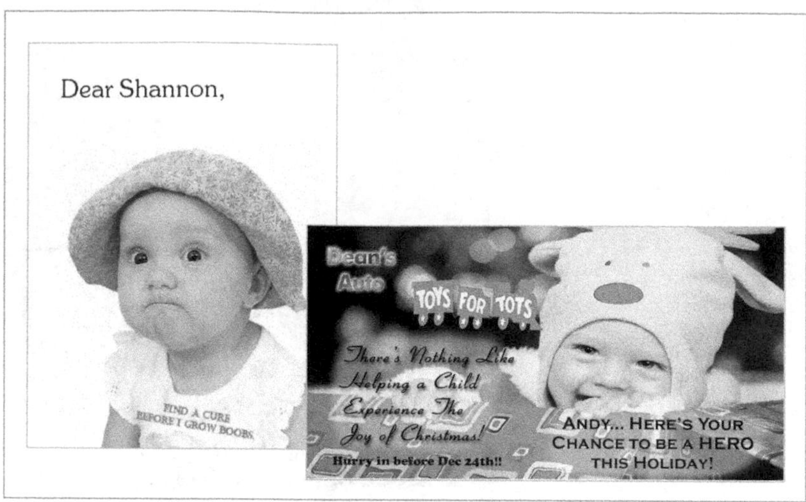

Create Your Own Occasions

If you're looking for what LEB/S are interested in, just ask them! A cause I personally support is the American Cancer Society. I lost my first wife to ovarian cancer, as well as my father and brother to prostate cancer. Needless to say, I am a big supporter of cancer research. How about Alzheimer's Awareness? I'm sure all of us LEB/S know someone who's affected by this terrible disease, guaranteed. For a list of all causes or holidays go to www.newcustomersnowmarketing.com/eventcalendar.

Contact Dean

For more information and to contact Dean personally, go to www.newcustomersnowmarketing.com/contactus.

Dean Killingbeck is a popular speaker, marketing consultant, and copywriter specializing in new customer acquisition for over 32 different business types. He also contributed to Dan Kennedy's *No B.S. Price Strategy* book, and his direct mailers have been shown as examples in *Dan's No B.S. Marketing to the*

Affluent Letter, The Ultimate Sales Letter book, as well as the *No B.S. Grass Roots Marketing* book. Dean is the owner of New Customers Now, a completely done-for-you producer of event marketing direct-mail pieces that drive new and existing customers through the client's doors. For a FREE event calendar or to contact Dean, go to www.EventMarketingForYou.com, or contact Shannon at (517) 548-5315 or Shannon@m2ncn.com.

CHAPTER 19

The Power of Aspiration and Ambition

Dan Kennedy

LEB/S have been about ambition.

Those coming behind are seriously questioning the LEB/S concept of ambition, and there is some pandering to their doubts. In a 2012 commencement speech, media personality, Kennedy family member, and Schwarzenegger ex-wife Maria Shriver advised college graduates that it was perfectly okay to emerge unsure of just about anything including what they might want to do with their careers or to earn a living (all but issuing permission slips to move back in with parents and relax), and promoting what she called "the pause"—the virtue of pausing *often* in life, in work, to ponder and reflect. The dearth of jobs for young people, including college graduates, blamed on the recession, and broad disillusionment with the

American economy coupled with overly tolerant parents are all contributing to malaise. The youngest newly minted adults are the first generation ever to not even bother getting their driver's licenses at the first available moment, opting for life on Facebook and the couch as an acceptable alternative.

Such ideas are foreign to LEB/S. Seniors and most LE-boomers have been engaged in "racing to the top" their whole lives. In upward mobility. In goal setting. The 1970s were the prime years of the personal growth and human potential movement in America—seminars and workshops on every corner as if convenience stores—and boom years here for the multilevel network marketing industry, led by already old dogs like Amway, and newer emerging titans like Herbalife, enticing millions of people every week into "opportunity meetings" in hotel ballrooms, pancake house back rooms, and living rooms coast to coast. Herbalife even, at one point, aired a multi-hour opportunity meeting and success rally live on cable TV every Sunday night. The concept of "Nothing Down" real estate investing hit its prime, too. At peak, an estimated 25% of the adult U.S. population was involved in a multilevel marketing operation, attending get-rich-in-"nothing down" real estate trainings, or spending weekends at "success seminars," or all three. Leading-edge boomers were right smack in the thick of it all, driving it with their ambition to be smarter, faster, more self-actualized, richer. Seniors lived their own bigger-is-better goal-oriented pursuit of the brass ring in the post-WWII boom. Hardly anybody was content just to be. The phrase "keeping up with the Joneses" was born as their ambitious behavior translated into the purchases of bigger homes with bigger yards, bigger cars, backyard swimming pools, vacation cottages, boats, RVs.

Combined, as a force of nature for the economy, LEB/S pushed the wave of optimism and conspicuous consumption that marked the '80s. After the brief down years with the dour-faced Jimmy Carter telling everybody to turn down their thermostats and wear sweaters, Ronald Reagan re-ignited the Grand Ambition of LEB/S, with his sunny personality, his trickle-down economics, and dramatic tax rate cuts not seen since JFK; tax cuts that said: *Spend!*

All this is important in understanding the LEB/S mind-set. We are, at this point, hard-wired, compulsive achievers. Required to set, pursue, and achieve goals, to crystallize and pursue ambition.

Just as an entire suburbia migration and lifestyle and all its accoutrements and large, luxury cars were sold to the seniors by tying to ambition, and just as racing to the top, second-income entrepreneurship in multilevel marketing, immigration from other fields to Wall Street was sold to LE-boomers by tying to ambition, we can now find exceptionally profitable opportunity in tying to whatever the new ambitions of LEB/S are.

The "2010 Del Webb Baby Boomer Survey" hands us their *new* ambition list. The two areas of life that LE-boomers want to improve in are—drum roll, please—physical health, cited as #1 by 35%, and financial security, cited as #1 by 25%. Their improvement goals are to (finally, now that they have time) get their act together with regard to their health or their personal finances. Or both. Further down in the rankings: repairing, improving, and strengthening relationships with family and friends (9%), achieving upward movement in career or business (6%), improving spirituality (12%), more time into and getting better at recreation/leisure activities (10%). Were I you, if interested in tapping the spending power of boomers, I'd be sitting down and trying to figure out how I could link myself, my business, my products and services to these ambitions, preferably #1 and/or #2, or how to reinvent so I could do so.

The AARP research showed that older seniors reveal more "measured perspective." What this means is that their ambition is more tempered. While generally optimistic about the future, they are more cautious in setting clearly defined goals, as their longer span of life experience and knowledge of reoccurring history tells them that things may not work out as planned. In the survey, a large percentage of those 65 and over described their attitudes toward the future as hopeful *and* anxious, confident *and* uncertain. This is not so much addled conflict as it is measured perspective. This gives us guidance in how to talk a little differently to seniors about ambition than to LE-boomers.

This does not preclude them enunciating ambition. Asked, in the same survey, what they want to spend money on and do, travel/more travel ranks highest at 18%, retirement at 12%, improve health at 13%, improve finances at 10%, all others down in single digits. Anyone in the travel field can do a happy dance. But this also suggests the kind of premiums and rewards to focus on: travel. And it suggests not putting as much emphasis on having more free time, more time with family, more time with grandkids as many advertisers do—these do not rank as major ambitions. They do rank high in expectation: 80% said they expected to spend more time with loved ones. Only 9% gave it chief ambition status.

I'll now remind you of the most time-honored formula for getting rich through marketing. It was once stated as "Find a need and fill it," but that required a bit of updating, as greater and greater percentages of our population had their basic needs met. In many product and service categories now, there are arguably no unmet needs. After all, if you need a cup of coffee or a doughnut or cupcake, you need not travel downtown or across town to *the* coffee shop or *the* bakery. Many goods and services once priced beyond reach of the masses are now fully democratized. Seniors will remember commercial air travel as a romantic luxury few could afford. As a young child, I was put on a Trailways bus to go from

Cleveland to Pittsburgh, to visit relatives; the idea of going by air was outrageous. Today, Southwest Airlines will fly you across country for bus fare. And so on. So, Zig Ziglar's admonition, taught from the '60s forward, better applies: "If you will help enough other people get what they *want*, you will certainly get whatever you want."

On this premise, dare we make opportunity predictions?

There is the Jewish proverb: If you wish to hear God laugh, tell him of your plans. Still, as business leaders we must attempt reasoned and psychic prediction, and we must attempt to plan and develop strategy, to at least stay apace with the most profitable buyers, if not a step or two ahead. With that in mind, here are a few predictions:

1. **LE-boomers are going to remain in family leadership for some time to come.** John Martin, CEO of The Boomer Project, says that boomers lead more households than any other generation, and now they are at the helm, often reluctantly, of more multi-generational households than ever before. Close to 16% of the American population now inhabit three-generation households, and almost all are headed by boomers. The TV show *Modern Family* portrays a version of this. There are certainly more TV shows of this ilk coming, as TV tends to mirror its viewers. This means, for some years to come, the boomer will be at the epicenter of household, financial, health-care, and other decisions for his own family, his boomerang adult kids moved back in, his senior parents also moved in. This may not be cheery news for some industries, like real estate, but it suggests adaptations by many industries—home remodeling leaps to mind—to capitalize, and a whole new field of multifamily household services and family-leader support services. Family therapists, life coaches, a new wave

of personal growth seminars, a spate of self-help books, a new kind of financial planner, etc., etc.; new designs in refrigerators, garage storage, what else?

2. **Dragged, kicking and screaming, or seeking ways to ease life's burdens, or seeking new social and entertainment options, Martin also predicts that LEB/S will get more and more wired.** I expect this to be pushed forward as physical-world services become less and less available and bear surcharges, compelling and even forcing acceptance of online services. The erasure of service and shift to self-serve was a gradual process that began with the first serve-yourself grocery store chain, Piggly-Wiggly®, in 1916, and picked up speed as service stations disappeared and the public was forced to pump its own gas, to the present, where we are asked to check ourselves out at the supermarket, make our own airline reservations online and check ourselves in at the airport, and vacuum out our own cars at the car wash, after depositing coins in a machine for the privilege. LE-boomers dislike some of these conversions from service to do-it-yourself, while the youngest boomers are more accepting, and the next younger people grew up with them and think nothing of them. Seniors dislike them most, naturally. In a very similar way, LEB/S will be guided into acceptance, grudging or not, of conducting their business, doing their banking, interacting with their doctors, and much, much more online. It will happen slower than corporate and government entities would like, but faster than most of these consumers would prefer—and there will be opportunity in being last-men-standing, delivering access to humans and personal service, for a while. The growth in LEB/S use of online social networks topped 80% from 2009 to 2011. The number of LEB/S users of Facebook leapt from about

one million in 2009 to over 12 million in 2011, according to Pew Research and iStrategy.com. This, too, has been largely forced, by adult kids and grandkids, and in some cases, business peers refusing to communicate by other means. Once dragged to it, many LEB/S users embrace it for more than the single purpose they were required to use it for; others do not. Still, I predict that the most productive, profitable driving forces in marketing to the LEB/S market for many years to come will continue to be offline media, with increased reliance on direct mail, as other print media is less and less available.

3. **Martin predicts that "health and wellness care will be everywhere."** That is obvious on its face. The real questions have to do with access; and with who will be delivering the care. My own view is that the current trends of consolidation and the absorption of small, independent providers into far fewer, big corporate-owned conglomerates already occurring in health care in the hospital and medical practice arenas will accelerate. I anticipate hospitals taking over a myriad of peripheral health-care businesses, such as dentistry and even chiropractic. Out the back end of it will likely come a fresh wave of fragmentation and new business format invention, but that is a decade away. To his "everywhere" prediction, there's no doubt that "low-end" health care is going retail. CVS, Walmart and others are already delivering certain kinds of medical care in their pharmacies and stores. The Association of Medical Colleges has warned of a shortage of as many as 90,000 doctors by 2020, and a growing disinclination toward general medicine or geriatric medicine by students and graduates, due to limits and likely cuts in Medicare reimbursements, other limitations built into "Obamacare," and an overall income disadvantage of at least $100,000.00 a year vs. other categories

of medical practice. Given growing doctor shortages and increasing pressure for cost control, more and more medical care will be pushed downstream, to nurse practitioners, mini-practices inside retailers' locations, in mobile-van and in-home practices and via online, where diagnosis and issuance of prescriptions is an evolving business very near the tipping point of a boom.

The Age-Profit Boom will also dramatically change the health club and gym industry. Already, the fastest growing consumer demographic buying memberships is 50 years old—and over. The industry is fast developing products, services, and classes for LEB/S consumers more interested in vitality than ripped abs, rock-hard bodies, or bulging muscles.

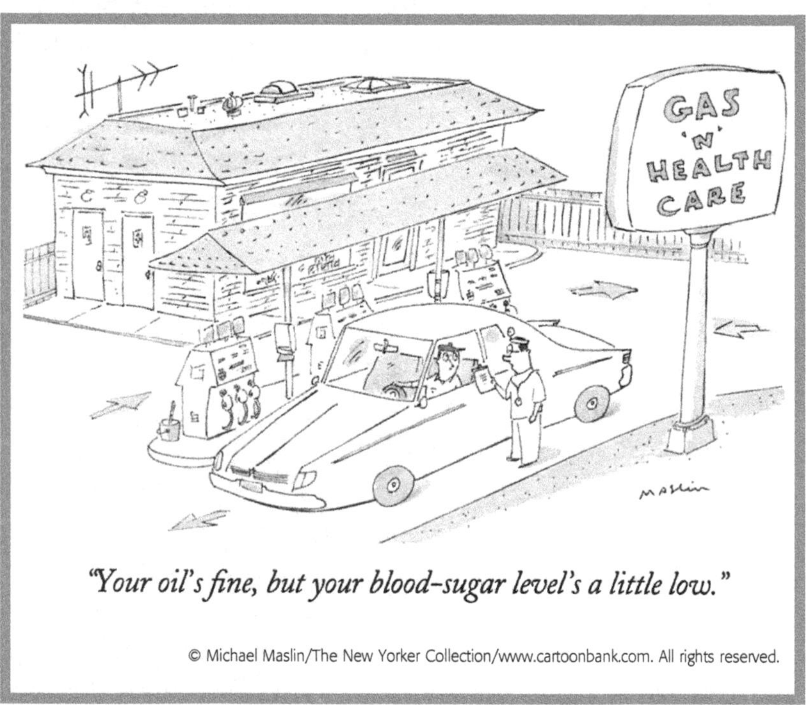

"Your oil's fine, but your blood-sugar level's a little low."

4. **I think that health-care centerpiece retirement communities are the coming trend.** If you recall from the start of the book, the "2010 Baby Boomer Survey" conducted by Del Webb, the king of retirement communities, showed that a warm, sunny climate was not the #1 concern—instead it was cost of living and access to health care. I live in a community now that has small townhouse clusters at its perimeter, large freestanding homes in its main neighborhoods, and maintenance-free cluster homes, both freestanding and duplex, in side neighborhoods. Celebration, the Florida community originally Imagineered by Disney, has apartments and townhouses at its edges, cluster homes, large freestanding homes, and very upscale mansion-like homes in segregated but connected neighborhoods, with a Main Street and small-townish Public Square as its centerpiece. Many upscale retirement communities are built with golf course and country club as their centerpiece, a design a client of mine years back, Florida Communities, copied in miniature scale, with a nine-hole short course, small lake, small lakeside clubhouse, and modestly priced premanufactured homes surrounding it all. I think the coming communities built for seniors will mimic these kinds of designs, but with a hospital campus—with hospital, geriatric E.R., every kind of health-care practice and assisted living facility also likely owned by the hospital—at its center instead of the country club or the mixed-use shopping streets.
5. **Opportunities in the "Independent Living Industry" will grow explosively and expansively.** Fifty-seven percent of Americans older than 65, polled by LifeGoesStrong.com and the Associated Press, said they were "very" or "extremely" likely to stay in their current homes, living independently throughout their retirement. The 57%

probably includes some overly optimistic folks, and omits quite a few resigned to other fates but who would profoundly prefer independent living in their own homes, were it possible. We need to find ways to facilitate this aspiration for socio-economic reasons. As the senior population surges and life span extends, the underlying Ponzi scheme not just within Social Security and Medicare, but of our entire economy is exposed. There cannot be enough new money to be taxed, taken, and redistributed to fund the retirement, health care, and nursing home/assisted living costs of the senior population, with those services constituted as they presently are. Some state governors, like Governor Kasich in Ohio, are pushing hard to reformulate state programs like Medicaid to provide more flexibility in paying for home health care, simply because it can be far less costly to assist a person staying in their own home than housing them institutionally for life. Of course, as marketers, we aren't focused on the needy, but on the big number who have financial capability to pay for their own enhanced quality of life. But know that staying at home and living independently is a huge motivational factor for the majority of seniors as well as the entire LEB/S population. It will be a fortune-making force for a great many entrepreneurs.

One of the fastest growth, opportunity-rich, ill-defined industries ever is and will be what I'm calling "the independent living industry," where products and services devoted to supporting seniors in living on their own their entire lives will converge and synergistically integrate in new ways, and entirely new businesses or modes of conducting business will rise up.

Technologies for "aging in place" is a $2 billion market now, but is projected to exceed $20 billion by 2020, according to Laurie Orlov, head of a Washington think tank studying the field. Jon Pynoos, a professor of gerontology at the University of Southern California, views the $20 billion projection as "optimistic but not unreasonable." He predicts more technology built into houses and more portable technology. The portable products to date are mostly improvements on the classic Life Alert, "I've Fallen And I Can't Get Up" button. But now that we have phones that talk to you, find restaurants that will deliver tomato soup for you, and direct you step by step to the nearest Starbucks, services to remind taking of medications at precise times, direct doctor-to-device monitoring (as with embedded pacemakers), permitting adult children to easily monitor parents' activity in their homes at a distance, etc., are fast emerging and gaining traction in the marketplace.

A company in this field called Rest Assured (www.restassuredsystem.com) marries in-home video safety monitoring (i.e., surveillance—and an array of electronic sensors) to watch over how long a senior has stayed in the bathroom or if they've opened their medicine cabinet at the correct times—with "Tele-Caregivers" who check in with the seniors several times a day. This approach entered test marketing only recently, and is in several hundred homes. I see no reason that both a business of Tele-Caregivers alone, as well as a high-tech/human touch hybrid like Rest Assured won't turn into growth categories. Yes, this does sound a little Orwellian. But sacrifice of privacy to stay out of nursing homes, assisted living centers, or the spare room in the kids' house will prove a price LEBs turning into seniors will be willing to pay.

In the pseudo-tech area, one of the front-runners is a direct marketing company, FirstStreet, with mail-order and online catalogs devoted to convenience products for seniors, notably the Jitterbug Phone and a proprietary, senior-friendly computer with limited, simplified internet capabilities, the ads for which can be seen online at www.FirstStreetonline.com. Studying this company is very instructive. Manufacturers of virtually any and every kind of product would be well advised to follow the yellow brick road paved by the Jitterbug Phone, and create senior-friendly versions of their products. The auto industry is doing it, without announcing it or positioning it as such, with cars that slam on their own brakes if backing into an object, park themselves in tight parking places, and give verbal directions to destinations.

Another of my clients, Paul Davey, a veteran owner of construction companies, has converted his firm to Independent Lifestyle Designs, specializing in any and all home makeover installations and modifications to facilitate seniors remaining safely in their own homes. His clients include government agencies, real estate investors, seniors, and the adult children of seniors. He has developed a referral network of hospital and rehab center administrators, doctors, social workers, and real estate agents. In one local area, while most contractors and remodelers have suffered at the hands of the recession, his business has achieved multimillion dollar year-to-year growth, and he has begun sharing his system with other construction and home remodeling business owners throughout the country (www.ILDNY.com). I believe that the consolidation of the products supporting in-home independent living like stair-lifts, walk-in tubs and showers, elevated toilets, security systems, etc., handicapped access home conversions, and full remodeling services in one "expert, trusted advisor" business is going to make fortunes for those participating in this business.

Silver-Ride, in San Francisco (www.silverride.com), is one of a burgeoning number of on-call transportation services that takes the elderly hither and yon, professionally and safely. With more than 70,000 trips so far, the company's been called on to provide car service for routine trips to the grocery store, late-night runs to 24-hour Walgreens, nights out to the opera, and every other imaginable purpose. The business is complicated by federal and state regulations and insurance requirements having to do with caring for seniors, such as certain first-aid training and certifications required for drivers, handicap accessibility equipped vehicles and the like. But what was once mostly the province of ordinary taxicab companies is fast becoming a specialty business. I recently read of a gerontology dentist closing her brick-and-mortar practice and creating a mobile dental care service for senior patients. Franchisors are invading the home health-care field in increasing numbers. I foresee a growing diversity of to-the-home and taking-seniors-out, individually and in groups, on outings businesses developing.

6. **Financial advice and legal advice will be major growth categories**, with clients willing to pay fees for services, for existing and new kinds of services. A client of mine, Bill Hammond, has pioneered a new subspecialty of elder law, called Alzheimer's law, for the needs of families in which an elder has been diagnosed with or is exhibiting worrying signs of Alzheimer's. He has not only built a hugely successful practice of his own, but has created a nationwide network of thousands of attorneys using his technical work, procedures, marketing, consumer education, and community outreach materials and methods (www.kcelderlaw.com). In Chapter 21 in this book, you can see the brilliant marketing of one of the top elder law

attorneys and business coaches to other elder law attorneys, Julieanne Steinbacher.

7. **The convergence of marketing to the affluent and marketing to LEB/S will escalate**. I am invested in a company, Tuscan Gardens, engaged in the development of small, boutique retirement communities with small but very upscale freestanding homes, nestled together in close quarters, with quasi-assisted living and medical services on site (www.TuscanGardens.com). I am invested in Kennedy's Barber Clubs, a classic men's shop with upscale club environment, featuring straight razor shaves, and operated on a membership rather than fee-for-service model (www.KennedysBarberClubs.com). It is squarely aimed at an affluent LEB/S clientele, with monthly membership dues above a hundred dollars. It has grown slowly but steadily during a recession launch to 13 successful locations, and is projected to at least double in number of units by year-end 2012. I made these speculative investments in startup companies with the conviction that businesses very specifically crafted for the affluent LEB/S offer some of the best growth, margin, and value opportunity for the remainder of this decade and well into the next.

   Concierges for the affluent LEB/S will grow in popularity and create new categories. Concierge medicine is already significant, and will only become more appealing should "Obamacare" or some reconstituted version of socialized medicine proceed. I predict the "home concierge" idea will come of age—the handyman, repair, routine maintenance, lawn care, watering of plants when owner's away, etc.—services all in the hands of one concierge. Or the "food concierge," who does the grocery shopping, restocking refrigerator and pantry, and prepares certain meals.

8. **LEB/S will re-assert itself as *the* target market for consumer brands, all sorts of products and services, entertainment, and more.** In 2010, LEB/S consumers spent about $1.3 trillion *more* than Gen X and Millennial consumers combined. Advertisers have been shifting focus, often clumsily. It's now common to see cosmetic and beauty ads in fashion magazines and on TV showcasing "women of a certain age" in place of the young, bold, and hopelessly beautiful. In 2012, Toyota brought forward TV ads presenting a particular car as for the LE-boomers, and not for younger customers. The TV soap opera all but disappeared in the networks' misguided making their main characters younger and younger, leaving their loyal audience behind but failing to attract the coveted young viewers, even as CBS took prime-time dominance with shows chosen for their appeal to LE-boomers, like *NCIS, Hawaii Five-O, Blue Bloods,* and *Dancing with the Stars*. Robert Downey, Jr., the actor best known at the moment as *Iron Man,* has reportedly acquired movie rights to a decidedly LEB/S character: Perry Mason. Las Vegas wounded itself with its recrafting for the very young. They got visitor counts up, but brought net profitability down. As a sign of their times, a liquor store is opening in the baggage claim area of the airport, so young people can stock up to drink in their rooms before hitting the clubs at night, thus reducing their bar tabs. I believe this will all sort itself out at a now accelerated pace, with advertisers and media aggressively re-engaging with LEB/S.
9. **"Made in America" may make a big comeback.** The global economy isn't going to diminish in importance, but I am tracking—more anecdotally than statistically at this point—a growing aversion to imported goods in many categories, particularly when logic says there should be

made-in-America available. I have personal bias here, so, a quick story. A huge box of Harry & David fruit arrived as a gift from a client. My wife and I opened it on the kitchen counter, read the glowing prose about the wondrous Harry & David orchards in Washington state or Oregon, I forget which, and how the seeds for these special pears were first brought there from France, etc., etc., etc. Then, just before unpacking the fruit, we spotted the little label: PRODUCT OF CHILE. I have nothing against Chile *per se,* and I intellectually know that they used very careful wording to skirt past an outright lie, but we still felt deceived, disappointed, and incredulous that pricey Harry & David specialty fruit was being lugged over here from beyond our borders. And we threw it out. And I made a note never to, myself, order anything from Harry & David. It is my opinion that manufacturers and sellers of goods that are home-grown, that are made in America, should promote that fact more boldly and emphatically than seems common, and I believe it gifts some price elasticity. I think the backlash from a likely long-standing if not permanent unemployment rate at 8% or higher—due to a variety of factors—will be a new isolationism, patriotism, and disapproval of companies exporting jobs and importing goods. There may even be new tariffs and trade wars and taxes tied to this, unwinding the dramatic opening of unfair trade from the Clinton administration.

These are just some of the key areas of opportunity that I'm talking about with my clients, researching and paying attention to for GKIC Members, and considering in my own investment activity.

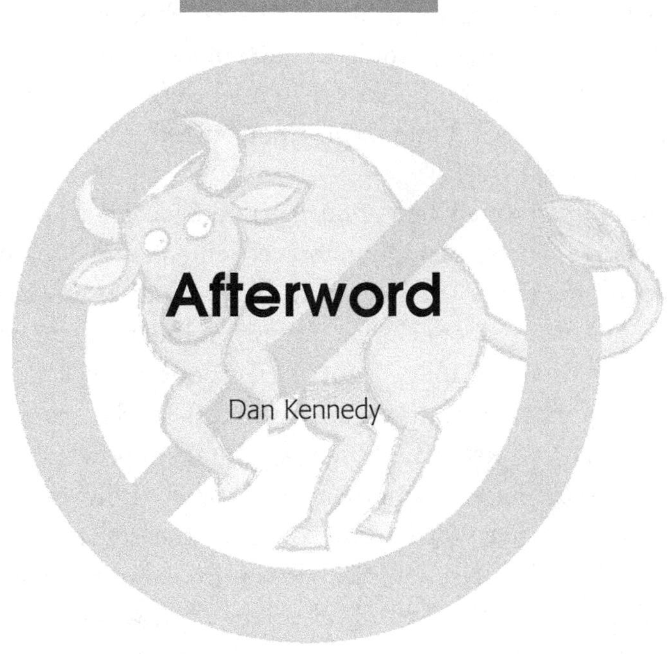

Afterword

Dan Kennedy

It is a popular idea among Gen X and Millennials that there is no longer any need for books. That this object you hold in your hands, with hopefully highlighted and scribbled notes and dog-eared pages, that you will return to more than once, is positively prehistoric. We can save the trees, shutter the libraries, even live in smaller houses, and wipe the landscape free of bookstores, replacing the entire clumsy, costly mess with the Kindle or the Nook or the iPad.

Know that the LEB/S consumer is not quite ready.

A small, independent bookstore on the main street of one of the handful of small towns that comprise my area of residence has been there since I was in high school. It is hopelessly overstuffed and cluttered. Three floors of a house converted to store.

Books on shelves, books on tables, books in stacks from floor to ceiling. There is even an aging, lazy bookstore dog, often sprawled on the floor, requiring customers to gingerly step over him. I first sold to this bookstore in my brief stint as a publisher's territory rep in 1973 and 1974. I patronized it as a customer as recently as last week.

Recently, a small item appeared in the local newspaper about this shop's owner readying for retirement and looking for a buyer for the store. The independent bookshop is an endangered species. Amazon looms large. Buying an independent bookstore is clearly financial folly. I got there about a week after I was told of the news item, prepared to invest six figures if need be, as a partner, to keep the little store intact and keep its present managers in place. Five others had come before me, with the same idea. What will become of it, in the short term, I can't predict. It is certain it will disappear into memory at some point. But at least six affluent LEB/S patrons are willing to open up their checkbooks and invest in a business guaranteed to die, to forestall the inevitable.

Isn't this an amazing thing?

Not to me. I know we are not alone. Far from it. The LEB/S folks are far from ready to let go of independently owned shops, of main streets in small towns, of real service by real humans in our real communities, of books, newspapers, letters in the mail, of TV shows absent gross humor and blatant sex, of patriotism and the idea of American exceptionalism, of shopping with a stack of paper and ink catalogs ensconced in a comfortable chair—not squinting at a computer screen; of filling out a paper and ink order form—not doing all that work then having it go "poof" and crash when the Buy Button is hit; of taking a real walk—not a virtual one; of talking with real friends at a real diner—not virtual friends, texted; of visiting a farm to buy fresh produce—not buying fake produce in Farmville. Not only is the

LEB/S group less willing than any previous generation to accept aging gracefully, to accept being put out to pasture and into nursing homes, to get the hell out of the way, LEB/S folks are not willing to be herded let alone stampeded into a new world shrunken to the size of a smartphone screen.

As is almost always the case, there are enormous amounts of money to be made with a contrarian approach. If you wish to view it as staying behind with the old folks, I guess, so be it, but there is a whole lot of 'em who still want *a book*.

The bookstore dog is old. A senior. Sleeping more, dreaming more, but doing less. With luck, he will not live to see the demise of his place, where friends he has come to know, perhaps more by smell than blurry sight, drop in to visit, chat, stroke his head, sometimes bring treats. Where the warmth of late spring and early fall days enters through the open shop doors to ease his aches, where the winter chill enters with each customer's arrival, to wake him from slumber so he misses nothing of interest. His Paris café where, if he sits there long enough, everyone passes by. With luck, he will pass peacefully on to a safer, peaceful place before witnessing destruction.

It is said that all progress is a product of destruction. Perhaps that is so. But the wisdom that comes only with age cautions that all destruction is not progress.

SECTION 3

BUSINESSES BUILT FOR LEB/S

THE GREAT MARKETING EXAMPLES in the following special guest contributors' chapters are from different businesses very successfully target marketing to LEB/S. Do not let the fact that you are not in the same product or service category as these grant you permission not to study them and think about their lessons. You can make a quantum leap up in income—and this is a chief premise underlying all my teaching—from the realization that your deliverables are *not* your business. You are in the marketing business *exactly the same as* these business owners are.

These guest contributors are all very active GKIC Members, and their marketing reflects GKIC influence and training. You can join them as Members on a free trial basis with the offer on page 264.

CHAPTER 20

Challenge of Selling What No One Wants

Case History: Nursing Home and Assisted Living (Health Care)

Chip Kessler

My primary business is health care. For the past ten years, I've actively served as a consultant for a select group of nursing-home clients in multiple states. A great deal of my time is spent guiding these nursing facilities in their marketing efforts. In addition, I oversee the day-to-day operations of a company that creates, develops, and produces staff development and training programs for those who work in our nation's nursing homes and assisted-living communities. To date, I've personally created 21 such programs consisting of DVDs, CDs, and various study guides. I'm pleased to report that there are nursing homes and assisted living communities in all 50 states utilizing these programs. First and foremost is a series of marketing programs to help nursing facilities attract new residents through their doors. In the vernacular of nursing homes, this is called "building census."

A Tough Marketing Challenge

Here's the rub: Nursing homes are marketing something that for the most part nobody wants! Think about it. Did you wake up this morning and have an overwhelming urge hit you . . . *I want to go live in a nursing home?* Hardly. Yes, it's a vitally important business, taking care of a group of our citizens who can no longer take care of themselves. So in this manner, a harried daughter, or a family in general, who can no longer provide competent care for their 83-year-old mother, father, or grandparent because he or she keeps falling or has a bad case of dementia, find the nursing home a godsend. Ask any senior, however, if he or she wishes to move into a nursing home and you'll get quite a different reaction. In fact, sometime in the past, the mother, father, or grandparent may have made the daughter or son promise to never put them into a nursing home, and now the children (probably baby boomers too) have to go back on their word because it's the best option for the situation at hand.

This is the marketing challenge nursing homes face.

The same is true for assisted-living facilities, though with their more hands-off approach to caregiving, assisted living doesn't quite carry the stigma nursing homes do. Ever been to an assisted-living community? Many look like hotels. Nursing homes, in many cases, come off looking like hospitals.

Speaking of hospitals, they are in much the same boat as nursing homes. Did you say to yourself today: *I've got to get the oil changed in my car, run out to the hardware store to buy a new tape measure, and then I've got to remember to check myself into the hospital because I've missed the enjoyment of staying there?*

That isn't happening today, is it?

Let's add doctors to this list. Basically any kind of doctor here, save the cosmetic surgeon who you may look forward to seeing in anticipation of your improved appearance. But who sees the fun of going in for a colonoscopy?

Dentists, ditto. Root canal. I've had a couple, no fun. Yes, you feel better afterward, so the result of such trips to the dentist (or in some cases a doctor or a hospital) has a successful end to the means; however, given any option, all still get a resounding thumbs down on a potential visit.

So when it comes to health care in general, we've established that the field is starting behind the marketing eight ball, but at least when we see such a trip to the hospital, doctor, or dentist as being unavoidable we can focus on feeling and getting better and the thrill of going home. Not so with nursing homes. Most people (save if you are there for some short-term rehab or a temporary condition) aren't leaving a nursing home, unless it means your body is headed to the funeral home!

Yet market we must, and market we do! And when it comes to marketing (and doing it well) to the prime category of baby boomers who have elderly parents, it is the difference between a thriving nursing facility and a building struggling to pay its bills and laying off its health care employees.

How to effectively do it? Plus how to do it in any health-care-related setting? Start with one word:

Trust

Let's start with nursing homes. The words "nursing home" send shivers down many people's spines. They're thought of by many as cold, uninviting places, populated by uncaring zombies who are there working just to cash a paycheck. The news media doesn't help. Think back to the last time you heard something about a local nursing home in the news, and more than likely it wasn't good—a case of alleged abuse or negligence, a lawsuit that was filed over this or some other situation, a fire, etc. Yes, these happen, but in far, far less proportion than the news media would lead you to believe. Fact is, there are thousands and thousands of outstanding people who work in our nation's nursing homes, doing a job that most of us aren't willing or capable of doing: providing care to a group of our fellow human beings who are no longer capable of taking care of themselves, whose families can't or won't provide this care. This is the marketing story we help promote for our clients.

"These caregivers do an unbelievable job," says Dr. Jon Ellis, Ph.D., a clinical psychologist who has vast experience working in nursing homes, and a welcome contributor to a stress management training program that is a key element in my brand-new *Nursing Facility Customer Service Survival Kit* staff development and education program. "These caregivers report to work each day with little fanfare. They have great hearts and a true desire to help others live the best quality of life possible."

In marketing brochures for my clients, such as Christian Care Center located in Kuttawa, Kentucky, we place reassuring photos of happy, smiling residents and staff members, a list of services and care provided, and we highlight benefits like these throughout the piece:

1. An understanding this is a tough decision and we are here to help you get through it.
2. Trained, professional staff for your loved one.
3. Encouragement to personalize the resident's room for a home-like feel.
4. Clean, caring environment.
5. The answer to your and your loved one's caregiving dilemma.

Consider the meanings within these lines of copy:

1. *Empathy*. As President Clinton said, "I feel your pain." People long to be *understood*. REASSURANCE. "We are here to help you get through it." There is implicit promise they *are* going to "get through it," that they will feel better, that there is light at the end of the tunnel.
2. *Feature/benefit made personal*. "For your loved one.
3. *Concern relief*. Everyone dreads a sterile, standardized, institutional room; a cell (!) with four gray walls.
4. *The essentials*. When describing your product, you should never take the basics for granted.
5. *Acknowledgement of reality*, a form of reassurance—we get that you have a "dilemma."

Dan is also a big proponent of marketing yourself as the "no-doubt-about-it, hands-down expert" in your field. This factor goes hand-in-hand in helping to build the trust factor, an especially vital ingredient when attempting to attract LEB/S to your goods, products, practice, or service.

So it is with nursing homes, and other health-care-related business. People want to place their mother or father in the nursing home that provides *expert* care. Do you come off as an expert?

Specialized Health Care for the Aging

Much as nursing homes and assisted living communities primarily serve a senior population (and some leading-edge boomers), there is a growing trend among other health-care practitioners to niche themselves to our increasing aging population, and thus they concentrate their marketing efforts on this expanding niche.

Physicians who specialize in seeing older patients (known as geriatric doctors) have been a fact of medical life for quite some time. Now, however, come several unique niches within the health-care world, all designed to capture the senior who is looking for specialized attention for their unique (so they believe) set of circumstances. In the April 10, 2012, edition of *The New York Times,* reporter Anemona Hartocollis' story "Geriatric Emergency Units Opening at U.S. hospitals" examines this growing trend. Here she tells of Mount Sinai Hospital in Manhattan now featuring an emergency room specifically geared to treating the medical needs of aging baby boomers and seniors. Mount Sinai reportedly modeled its geriatric emergency room after one opened at St. Joseph's Regional Medical Center in Patterson, New Jersey, back in 2009.

Ms. Hartocollis' piece traced the advent of such hospital emergency rooms even further, citing Holy Cross Hospital in Silver Springs, Maryland, as seeing this expanding need for senior care, and opening its geriatric emergency room in 2008. Reportedly, Trinity Health System, which operates 12 hospitals nationwide (predominantly in the Midwest) and is the parent company of Holy Cross Hospital, plans to open six or seven such geriatric emergency rooms in some of its facilities during 2012, according to the Hartocollis story.

What does this trend mean for the marketer looking to tap into the expanding baby boomer and senior populations, whether targeting your message to this group's health-care needs, or describing whatever your goods, products, and/or services are?

Namely, that this is a segment of our populace that you can't afford to ignore and can best capitalize on and be of service to by creating specialized products and services.

Hospital Marketing

Ever take some time to really study how hospitals market themselves? Here's generally what they don't spend too much time (and advertising dollars) doing in their TV, radio, newspaper, and other forms of marketing:

- How great the food is
- How comfortable the beds are
- How good the TV reception in your room is going to be

Instead, hospital marketing overwhelmingly goes back to that earlier word. Now let's take a look at what hospitals do marketing-wise, and see if you can figure out what that "word" is. Hospitals like to market and advertise:

- The Awards and Honors the Hospital Has Received for Outstanding Care
- Awards and Honors That a Particular Physician or Department Has Won
- Reminding You About Some Outstanding Features in the Building Such as a Level One Trauma Unit, New Cancer Treatment Center, or an Addition to Their Children's Hospital
- Personal Testimonials from a Discharged Patient's Success Story
- Personal Testimonials from a Discharged Patient's Family Member on How Wonderful the Hospital's Care Was and How It Led to Mother or Father Going Home

Know what the word is that I was earlier referring to?

T-R-U-S-T

Anything here you can swipe and deploy to make yourself more appealing to an age group of people who place a very high value on this characteristic?

With trust established, it can also be a very short trip to achieving the role of expert status in your chosen field, and, as already pointed out by Dan Kennedy, this is a major factor to winning the hearts and minds of a particular market that places a great deal of importance on these traits when determining who (and who not) to do business with.

Hospitals also do a very effective job of letting you know how much they are involved in your region and community, sponsoring or playing very visible and dominant roles (utilizing staff members wearing T-shirts or jackets bearing the hospital's name) in the following activities:

- The local 5k run
- Relay for Life®
- Sponsoring youth sports teams
- Signage at ball fields and school basketball gymnasiums
- Making donations to worthwhile charitable causes and community projects
- Encouraging staff members (again wearing hospital T-shirts and jackets) to participate in charitable and community projects
- Holding health fairs, blood drives, sponsoring a mobile unit giving free blood pressure checks, etc.

Hospitals take great pains to make sure you know they are a major presence and supporter of anything and everything that makes your region tick. It doesn't matter if the facility is operating in a town of 1,000 people or in New York City. While the former may have the entire town to demonstrate its community involvement, the latter (for the most part) takes its particular geographic locale into account and makes itself the dominant community presence.

Is there anything here for you to model, with regard to community events, to make you and/or your business or practice even more known as an indispensable entity? Sure, hospitals more than likely employ a great many more folks than you do, and thus have the luxury of calling on a tremendous flow of people, yet you can make up for this in your personal attention to those you are attempting to reach.

Notice anything in particular about the two bullet-point lists I jotted down for your review? Take a moment and re-read the lists of things that hospitals like to promote about their community involvement as well as the features and benefits you enjoy by going to their facility. One important aspect is missing. It's the same aspect of marketing that nursing homes don't get into as part of their marketing and advertising messages. For the most part, doctors and dentists don't either; even some chiropractors don't do it. It's price.

Why Price Doesn't Matter in Health Care and Shouldn't in Your Business or Practice

Here's an advertisement you won't ever see in your local newspaper or Yellow Pages; you won't see it if a local hospital is running a commercial on local TV or radio; it won't appear in a direct-mail piece, either, even in marketing to LEB/S:

> *The Loving Care Hospital Special for the Month of March: Heart Bypass Surgery at 50% off the Regular Rate! Coming in April: Get That Hernia Taken Care of and Save 65%*

If you did see such an advertisement, what are the chances that you'd be flocking down to the ol' XYZ Hospital and taking them up on their offer?

There are a couple of reasons why hospitals, and nursing homes for that matter, don't get into marketing and advertising price. Some reasons are of a substantial nature:

Insurance–Most of us (hopefully) have insurance that is going to pay for the large majority of that heart bypass operation. Yes, there may be some out-of-pocket expenses, but by and large we are looking to an outside source to cover most of the costs, so price doesn't really enter the equation.

Supplemental Insurance–Same scenario as just listed, only this policy takes care of the out-of-pocket expenses, so your hospital bill (despite those aspirin tablets at $35.00 a pop) is nothing but a large stack of papers you can file away.

Government–Based on the person's age (especially in the case of seniors and aging baby boomers), Medicare and Medicaid enter the picture and the state and federal government is involved in the fee. This is especially true in the case of nursing homes, where the large majority of these facilities work with Medicare and Medicaid to get reimbursed for the care and services provided. Medicaid is also a possibility to help pay for staying in an assisted living community, though not all states pay for such care.

Other Methods of Third-Party Payment–No need to list them all here; suffice it to say, however, that there are options such as long-term care insurance as well as numerous other third-party payment providers, which help pay for nursing home stays.

Contributor Chanel Adams on the website www.ehow.com writes about government grants being available through the U.S. Department of Health and Human Services (HHS), which offers some 300 grants programs, and awards some 75,000 grants per year. The elderly here are of special consideration, according to Adams, in receiving this financial assistance to pay for a long-term hospital stay. The report goes on to state how there is also a grant program for union members and retirees, and another grant program available for people with children.

Then there's the practical reason why hospitals, nursing homes, and physicians alike don't stress price in their marketing and advertising messages. Think back to my earlier "advertisement" for discounts on operations. If you saw a local hospital doing this, or let's say a local physician promoting a complete physical (including blood work) for the "low, low price of just $19.95," are you going to instantly call and make an appointment? I think not.

Price just isn't part of the deciding factor. You should feel the same way in promoting your goods, services, products, or programs. Nowhere is this more evident, for the most part, than in health-care marketing and advertising. The very idea of selecting your new doctor based on his or her rates is laughable. Boomers and seniors won't do it.

Indeed, certain professionals do market by price; however, you have to look at the clientele he or she is wishing to attract. Cases in point:

- The no-fault divorce attorney pushing a $99.00 special.
- The CPA promoting a "Do Your Taxes" $29.95 program.
- The Dentures establishment advertising a full mouth of new teeth for $129.95.

Chances are, whether it is a baby boomer, a senior, or someone of a younger nature, if he or she can afford it, they will be going someplace else. You never get the really good patients or clients with price.

Privately Speaking

As mentioned earlier, not all assisted-living communities accept state funding through Medicaid. Conversely, many residents pay for their stay out of their own pockets. All so-called retirement communities, also known in some circles as independent-living facilities, are completely what is labeled "private pay." Nursing homes, long a bastion of receiving Medicare and Medicaid payments to pay all or a large portion of a resident's stay, have also seen a slight shift.

Introducing the private-pay nursing home. Here, there are no third-party payment partners, just you. In fact, one of the nursing facility clients I consult with is getting ready to face some competition from a brand-new nursing home being constructed in their town—a private-pay facility, complete, I'm told, with a putting green. Think this new building is going to attempt to attract a specific kind of affluent clientele? Me, too! I'll be interested to see how the owners of this new facility present their building's marketing story to the public.

No doubt we needed to ramp up my client's marketing efforts, and as this is being written, we have already begun to do so.

How about your particular situation? Are you doing all that you can to separate yourself from the run-of-the-mill and the ordinary? Going after the high-end LEB/S is certainly one way to accomplish this, no matter what your business happens to be, health care or not. With nursing homes, assisted-living communities, and independent-living facilities all addressing the private-pay factor, some hospitals aren't far behind.

Memorial Hospital in Huntington, California goes as far as to list on its website (www.huntingtonhospital.com) its "Self-Pay Policy." Here the hospital actually goes against the trend and lists some of its fees, not as a discount hospital for its services but as a means of letting one know what they will be paying for.

Baby Boomers, Seniors, and the Power of Fear

In some of what I do marketing with my nursing-home clients, and particularly marketing via Extended Care Products in the promoting of the risk management and staff development/ training programs we sell, the subject of fear is often front and center. For example:

- In a *Crisis Communications* DVD program we have, I'm always promoting the fact that failing to plan is planning to fail. As a means of making my point, I've actually used the term "The Ostrich Syndrome" after our friend who sticks his head in the sand, oblivious to what is taking place.

I've referred to what took place at a particular Louisiana nursing home after Hurricane Katrina struck a few years back and how ill-prepared facility officials were to deal with the families of residents, the media, and local authorities.

To make my point about our *"Complete Crisis Communications Plan,"* I've brought up examples of fires and alleged abuse and negligence that have struck other nursing homes and assisted-living communities, driving home the point that it can happen to you. I've also gone outside the health-care realm and written about what took place in the Joe Paterno situation at Penn State as a textbook example of how not to handle a crisis. In other words, I use *fear* to say, "Don't let this happen to you," because of the potential fallout in litigation, finances, ruined reputation, etc.

Our signature DVD program is a family educational presentation titled *Setting Realistic Expectations.* Nursing facilities and assisted-living communities show it to new families during the admissions process and then give them a copy to share with other relatives and keep for future reference. It tells them about what life is like and the care and services provided in these health-care settings . . . and to have reasonable expectations. And while it is a "family educational" DVD, from the health care facility's point of view its main benefit is that the DVD helps prevent potential lawsuits from being filed against the building since the presentation explains why a loved one may still fall inside a nursing home. Here, the DVD says if a person has had a history of falls in their home before entering the nursing facility, he or she may still fall in the nursing home.

> Accordingly, the video presentation goes on to educate as to why other incidents may occur. After viewing, families understand that all their loved one's problems may not be solved simply because he or she is now in an assisted-living community or nursing home.
>
> The use of fear-based marketing with the *Setting Realistic Expectations* DVD is front and center: the fear of being sued; the fear of paying out thousands if not millions of dollars in a settlement or a judgment; the fear of your facility being plastered all over the local newspapers and TV stations because you're being sued.

These are just a couple of examples of how I use fear in marketing. The result is hundreds of thousands of these (and our other programs) being used in facilities in all 50 states.

How can fear be effectively used in other forms of marketing? Let me count some of the ways:

- Chiropractors who mention the fear of living with chronic back pain as a means of selling their services.
- Hair-replacement clinics that pitch men the fear of being shunned by the ladies for being bald (and of late, selling hair replacement for women utilizing the same fear of being ostracized by society because of your appearance).
- Insurers and insurance companies bring up the loss of personal property without getting duly compensated in case of a fire, burglary, etc., and for you to have adequate life insurance so that your loved ones are well looked after in case you die.
- Supplemental insurance companies, there for you to make sure that hospital stay doesn't bankrupt you.
- The security company demonstrating homes being broken into, property stolen or destroyed because you didn't have an alarm system in place.

- A product of the times (and what can be considered a cousin of the security system folks): the anti-identity-theft companies warning you that your identity can be compromised in the blink of an eye and your bank account pilfered if you don't have the proper protection.
- The weight-loss program promoting a slimmer, trimmer you and enjoying life all the more without fear of being overweight, afraid to wear that bathing suit in public and getting ridiculed.

What about you? Are you *properly scaring* your clients, customers, and patients (when necessary) to let them know that what you have is the answer to their concerns and worries? In particular, when it comes to marketing to LEB/S, fear can be a very effective tool. And no, I don't mean that you should look to scare them so bad that a 70-year-old grandmother is going to have a coronary because she fears that her wrinkled face is driving her relatives to shun her, or that a 66-year-old man is going to consider moving to the wilds of Canada to get away from civilization because you've inferred he's going to become a victim of identity theft. What I do mean is presenting a real, honest-to-goodness problem they are facing in a thoughtful insightful, manner—and that YOU HAVE THE SOLUTION!

Fear can be an ally here in driving home your message.

The website www.artinstitutes.edu in an article "The Four-Letter Word in Advertising: Fear" captures the mood perfectly, using as an example the well-known TV commercial showing a mother in the park with two kids: a baby in a stroller and a little boy named Kevin. The mother turns for a moment to tend to the baby, and when she turns back around, poof, Kevin has disappeared . . . indeed, every parent's nightmare.

Do you recall what this commercial was for? Nope, it's not a public service announcement on guarding against child predators, though that's the inference as to what happened to Kevin loud and clear. The commercial plays on with the mother reaching for her handbag, dumping everything out while frantically looking for something, which turns out to be a child-locating device that eventually leads her to Kevin, who is walking in another part of the park, carrying a red balloon.

So the commercial was for the child-locater device, a mother's best friend, correct? Wrong.

It was for batteries and specifically this particular type of battery that is so dependable that in "every parents' worst nightmare" the child-locater device works every time because the batteries placed inside it work without fail in a moment of crisis! This is an example of just how far some advertisers will go to connect their product with fear. Even though it's a big stretch, they try making it because they know fear is such a powerful motivator.

Figure 20.1 is a sample sales letter for a resource for the LEB facing the need to obtain care for a senior. You can see how it includes the marketing tactics I've described and that are described throughout the book.

FIGURE 20.1: Kessler Sales Letter Example

At-Home Healthcare … Specialized Care-at-Home … Adult Day Care …
Independent Living … Assisted Living … Nursing Home …

So many choices for care; how will you find the best fit?

Finally, Discover the Right Caregiving <u>Answer</u>
For Yourself, a Loved One, or a Very Special Friend
New Breakthrough DVD, Study Guide & Fact Finding Questionnaires
Eliminates All the Guesswork, Misunderstandings and Fear of the Unknown

Doesn't Your Husband, Wife, Mom, Dad, Grandmother or Grandfather,
A Very Special Friend in Your Life, or Even Yourself
<u>Deserve</u> the Finest Care Possible?

- At last … the Fastest and Easiest Way to Understand the Differences Between the Variety of Caregiving Options Out There
- Learn What Services At-Home Healthcare … Specialized Care-at-Home … Adult Day Care Centers … Independent Living Facilities … Assisted Living Communities … and Nursing Homes <u>Do and Don't Offer</u> to Find the Perfect Fit
- Become Comfortable and Confident as You Find Out More About "The Choices for Care" From the Ease of Your Home Whether it's for Yourself, a Loved One or a Special Friend
- Discover Your Caregiving Choices <u>Today</u> Rather Than Wait Until It's Too Late and Make the Wrong Decision … or Worse Leave the Choice to a Stranger

Hello!

I'd like to tell you a brief story. Like you, I was searching for information on what caregiving options were available and what each offered. In my case, I needed to discover these important facts for my aging Mother. Mom was still in fairly good health however I could see that at 83 years young, she was starting to need something. <u>The question: what?</u> You see Mom was now having trouble getting up the step to her apartment's front door, plus she was starting to forget things on a regular basis. I began to see a trend and was worried that she might slip and fall, or that she'd forget to turn the stove off after making herself a cup of coffee- Mom never did like to use a microwave and refused to let me buy her one!

FIGURE 20.1: Kessler Sales Letter Example, continued

Both my wife and I work full-time, so I knew that Mom would soon require someone or something to help keep an eye on her. Most importantly, I wanted Mom to be comfortable and to live out the rest of her days (hopefully years) with the respect and dignity she's earned, so whatever I decided had to be the right choice for her. And I'll tell you a secret ... **Mom's changing condition was a wake up call for me**. I realized that I didn't want to wait until the last minute and then scramble around because there was no time to lose. I wanted to learn about the world of caregiving and not feel pressured to have to make a decision or worse have someone at a hospital force-freed me caregiving information because Mom had become too much of a risk to be on her own any longer!

You see, not only Mom's life but all human life's important to me. I learned this first-hand several years ago when the airplane I was a passenger in crashed approximately 20 minutes after take-off. As the picture shows, it was a miracle I survived! It's equally stunning because all of the passengers and crew escaped the fire and smoke and lived to talk about it. As a result, I've come to treat each day as a gift.

With this thought in mind, I wanted to make sure that my Mother would receive just the right type of care for her special needs. I'm sure you feel the exact same way whether it's for yourself, a loved one, or a very special friend that's in need of a caregiving boost.

This said, wanting to find just the right "Choice for Care" for Mom wasn't easy. I soon discovered that there really wasn't much information available all in one place to help me compare one caregiving possibility to the next. My only alternative was to visit them all and personally speak to the people that would specifically be involved in my mother's care. Being on a mission, that's what I did!

Today I'm pleased to offer you the results of spending countless hours studying the various caregiving options available. Now, rather than you personally visiting <u>all</u> of the caregiving choices to see what may or may not work, I'm happy to save you the time and trouble and give you a head-start. I'm proud to introduce you to the "Choices for Care" program. As its name says, this program truly is a complete analysis of all caregiving options. You get the following power-packed information line-up:

- ✓ ***A Time for Care* DVD video program.** Filmed live at actual Independent Living, Assisted Living, Adult Day Care and Nursing Home facilities along with specific home healthcare settings, you won't get any closer to these exclusive environments ... unless you step into them yourself. Experience first-hand what

FIGURE 20.1: Kessler Sales Letter Example, continued

each particular caregiving option has to offer. Watch as actual residents and staff work together. You'll also discover:

- The detailed type of care and services each option does and doesn't make available
- The ability to compare and contrast what each caregiving choice presents
- What kind of government and third party payment opportunities each option allows
- And much, much more

After watching *A Time for Care* you'll enjoy:

- A better understanding of what caregiving selections are available for yourself, a loved one, or a valued friend
- The skill to pick what's the best potential choice or choices, plus the ability to eliminate the caregiving options that don't offer what's needed or wanted
- The knowledge and confidence you'll want to take the next step in deciding what caregiving possibility works best for your situation

✓ ***The Choices for Care Workbook and Study Guide.*** Here at your fingertips is a full presentation of the detailed information on the DVD. You can use this quick and handy reference anytime and anywhere in your efforts to discover the best caregiving opportunities available to meet the needs at-hand. You'll get:

- A point-by-point breakdown of what each caregiving choice has to offer.
- Additional material not found on the DVD to help further your education
- The luxury of referring time and again to this workbook-study guide whenever and wherever you need an important piece of information regarding your caregiving possibilities
- The perfect companion to the DVD program to give you added peace of mind in your caregiving journey

Plus for those of you coping with the guilt of potentially placing a loved one into a structured care environment, there's a very special chapter on dealing with guilt from my

FIGURE 20.1: Kessler Sales Letter Example, continued

book, *A Sacred Trust*. Here, you'll learn to understand why placing a spouse, a parent, a grandparent or a very special friend into a caregiving setting isn't selfish or unkind, but is actually the greatest form of love you can give.

"I can't possibly put into words what this caregiving program has given me. I was faced with doing something about my father's care and didn't know where to turn. Thank goodness I learned about 'Choices for Care'. The DVD is full of great information. It helped steer me to discover why either assisted living or a nursing home was best. I really liked the fact that you show actual scenes from all the caregiving choices because it really helped to see what they're like. Together with the written materials you provide, I was then ready to narrow down the process until as you say I found the right 'Choice for Care' for my Dad. Thank you from the bottom of my heart!"
Lucille Dugger, Plano, TX

Now is the Time to Take Charge of Your Situation

Whether it's for yourself, a treasured relative like your mother, father, grandparent, sister, brother, in-law, or a valued friend, there's never been a better time to discover the best caregiving option for your situation. Just imagine the pain and heartache (not to mention the pressure) if you're forced to scramble around at the very last minute because you or your special someone:

- Is checking out of the hospital and have been told it's not wise to live alone at home anymore because of a health concern ... what are you going to do now?
- Is in need of some sort of caregiving help because of repeated falls in the home ... what are your best options out there?
- Is not eating properly and/or forgetting to take medication at the proper times of the day ... what can be done?
- Is facing a specific healthcare crisis that demands you or a special person in your life needs professional caregiving help ... where do you go and where do you turn?

Why would you want to wait to the very last minute and then try to find out what's your best course of action?

<u>SPECIAL NOTICE:</u> Let me be frank because this is a subject that demands complete honesty. If the person is you or your spouse that's in need of caregiving, **don't you**

FIGURE 20.1: Kessler Sales Letter Example, continued

deserve to know as much as you can about the available choices out there? Now, you can make the right decision. **And if care's needed for your mother, father or grandparent don't you owe it to them to find the best option to meet the need at-hand?** Think back for a moment, when you were growing up wasn't Mom or Dad always there for you during the tough times ... did you ever have a bigger cheerleader than your Grandmother or Grandfather when you were a youngster?

Indeed we'd all like to picture our parents and/or grandparents as vital and full of life. Why wasn't it only yesterday that Dad was up at dawn with the birds and racing out the door to hit another day on the job, and Mom was humming in the kitchen as she was making your favorite breakfast? Think back to the excitement you felt during the ride to your Grandparent's house- why you just knew there'd been an extra piece of pie or cake if you asked and could get the Sunday funnies read to you! And yet it isn't yesterday anymore. It's today and there are some decisions to be made that shouldn't be pushed to the side because you might not want to face them. Wouldn't you prefer to get the facts and then make the right choice coolly and calmly ... rather than feel rushed and pressured and make the wrong decision! That's where *The Choices for Care* program can and will help.

Act Today to Invest in Your or Your Special Someone's Tomorrow
Save 33% and Get Two Bonus Gifts

For a very limited time get the *Choices for Care* DVD and study guide program for only $99.95 and save 33% off the regular investment of $199.95. Plus when you reserve your program, you'll get the following three free bonus gifts:

Bonus gift #1: We'll pay your shipping and handling expense, a $20 value.

Bonus gift #2: The *Choices for Care Personal Questionnaire©*. Developed exclusively for this package, this questionnaire helps eliminate the guesswork involved when identifying the best possible caregiving options for yourself or a very special person in your life. The questions are specifically designed to identify the level of care that's needed for the situation at-hand and eliminate confusion as you pinpoint the best potential choices. A $29.95 value, it's yours when you receive *Choices for Care.*

Be One of the First 29 People to Respond to This Opportunity
Before Monday at 11:59 p.m. and Get a Third Bonus Gift

Bonus gift #3: *The Choices for Care Facility/Agency Questionnaire©.* Now that you've indentified the best caregiving option(s) and eliminated others, what's your next step?

FIGURE 20.1: Kessler Sales Letter Example, continued

The answer is to find out as much as you can about the exact care and services a facility or agency will and won't provide. **This particular questionnaire is the finest document of its kind ever developed because it gives you specific information to make an educated decision.** Each caregiving option (at-home healthcare, specialized care-at-home, adult day care, independent living, assisted living, nursing home) is listed with its own specific and targeted group of questions for you to ask, whether you're visiting a caregiving facility or healthcare agency in-person, or calling via the phone. You're now comfortable in the process because you don't have to guess at what questions to ask, think on the fly, or worry that you might forget something to bring up. A $39.95 value, this very special questionnaire is yours when you say yes to the *Choices for Care* program.

- In all you get $89.90 in bonus gifts almost your total investment in the *Choices for Care* program if you act now.

"I was totally lost until I discovered Choices for Care. I believed that I needed some care assistance. My wife had passed away about a year ago, and I've been alone with no other family nearby. I really didn't know where to turn to find answers for what was best for me. However after watching the DVD and using the self-questionnaire I could see that the at-home healthcare option was perfect! Next, I went to the Yellow Pages and called two of the companies that advertised this kind of care and asked each of them the questions you supplied. It helped me to decide what company to meet. The care they provide have been outstanding and I wanted to write you this letter to express my gratitude.
Jerome V. Cummings, Sarasota, FL

Act now and get the "Choices for Care" Program at www.ChoicesforCare.com or call toll-free 1-888-206-2244. You may also send us your check (made out to Choices for Care) to: Choices for Care, P.O. Box 4852, Johnson City, TN 37602.

Get *Choices for Care* Today and Take a Full Month to Review It
If You Are Not Satisfied Return the Program for a Cheerful Refund

Receive the *Choices for Care* program and take 30 days from the time you receive it to watch the DVD, review the study guide and look over both the Personal Questionnaire along with the Facility/Agency Questionnaire. If during this time, you don't feel that the program will help you select just the right caregiving option for yourself, a loved one or a very special friend then return it for a complete refund ... no questions asked. Plus you may keep the workbook/study guide with my compliments for your time and trouble. What could be fairer?

FIGURE 20.1: Kessler Sales Letter Example, continued

As the saying goes, *"today's the first day of the rest of your life."* That's true whether it goes for you or a treasured person in your life. No matter who it is, all of us deserve to spend our days in comfort and with the dignity and respect we've earned. With *The Choices for Care* program, this isn't just a wish; it's a reality. Now for the first time you can discover all the facts about the various caregiving selections available and feel good about your final decision. After all, you and/or your special someone deserve it!

With my very best wishes for your successful caregiving journey,
Chip Kessler
Developer and Producer
Choices for Care

CHAPTER 21

A Creative Approach to Products vs. Services

Case History: Elder Law Practice

Julieanne E. Steinbacher and Adrianne J. Stahl

Our law firm is very successful because we know how to market to LEB/S. Ten years ago we started our elder law firm and have been marketing to and working with seniors every day since. Our firm focuses on long-term health-care planning, targeting LEB/S who are currently in need of long-term care in addition to those LEB/S who are healthy now, but want to plan ahead.

We started our elder law firm with only the two of us working out of the living room of one of our homes. Now our firm consists of over 20 employees, two office buildings, and a resource center. Our Elder & Special Needs Resource Center is open to the public, offering information about all levels of care, from skilled nursing care to assisted living to in-home care, and educating family caregivers and professionals about issues facing individuals who are aging or have a disability. We also coach elder law and estate planning attorneys from across the nation on how to market to LEB/S.

If any business is going to survive and thrive in today's economy, it must offer and effectively market products or services that LEB/S will buy.

Choosing to Present Services or Tangible Products

Entrepreneurs generally first create a product or service they want to sell and then identify their ideal consumer; however, because of the current and future size of the LEB/S populations, many entrepreneurs are identifying these populations as their target market first and then trying to come up with some thing or service that will be attractive to boomers and seniors.

A very valuable insight is that LEB/S differing life experiences influence whether these groups are more likely to buy a tangible product versus a service. Having lived through an economic depression, seniors are frugal. They value tangible goods, so, as attorneys providing high-value legal services as opposed to tangible products, we make sure our senior clients leave our office early on in our relationship with something tangible, such as a power of attorney document, even though this is not the real value of our services. Along these same lines, one of the reasons we provide our clients with a *written* long-term health-care plan, or roadmap, is so that our knowledge becomes something tangible that seniors more readily view as a valuable investment.

Boomers on the other hand are less interested in tangible things. They prefer services over products. They are more accustomed to paying for services, for hiring all sorts of things done for them rather than doing them for themselves (as seniors naturally—and frugally—would). We sell boomers expertise, service, and peace of mind, not legal documents. We are their trusted advisors. We offer them protection and prepare a roadmap to guide them through the maze of the aging network.

Avoidance of Pain

The first step in marketing any product or service is to identify your ideal market—is it seniors, older boomers, younger boomers? Which group is most likely to buy your product or service at a premium price? The second step in marketing your product or service is to develop a marketing campaign that directly targets your ideal consumer. In developing a marketing message, it is important to remember that the leading reason anyone buys anything is either to seek pleasure or avoid pain. Generally speaking, the majority of people have a stronger desire to avoid pain; however, to determine which desire is stronger within your target market, you'd be wise to consider your target customer's life experiences.

Given seniors' firsthand experience with suffering, such as the fear, starvation, and illness of the Great Depression, as a group they are frugal and desire to avoid pain. They are reluctant to spend money on themselves, particularly on a product or service that they perceive as a source of pleasure. Seniors feel obligated to save every penny they have for their children and grandchildren. This makes selling to seniors more difficult than selling to boomers.

Our senior clients have responded to marketing messages promoting the avoidance of pain, such as these:

- Don't Go Broke in a Nursing Home
- Don't Lose Your Home
- Don't Leave Your Spouse Penniless

As we described previously, LEB/S differing life experiences and even the various age groups within the categories of LEB/S color whether these groups are more likely to respond to one marketing message versus another. Those early, or aging, boomers, born from 1946 to 1955, grew up at a time when the economy was good; whereas the boomers born in the latter part of the baby boom grew up in a weaker economy. For this reason and the life experiences of boomers previously discussed, aging boomers tend to be more likely to seek pleasure, and younger boomers tend to be more likely to avoid pain.

Additionally, a major difference within the boomer group is that, given the 18-year span of the baby boom, boomers are now in varying stages of life. The oldest boomers are contemplating retirement and have adult children and grandchildren. Those born in the middle of the baby boom (1952–1958), otherwise known as the "sandwich generation," still have children at home and are caring for an aging parent. The youngest boomers are at their top earning years and have children still at home.

If you desire to target the boomer group as a whole, you may want to include both pain-avoidance and pleasure-seeking messaging within a single marketing piece. Furthermore, you may want to use a message that targets all of the varying life stages of boomers. For instance, in our ad for the "Free Seminar on Long-Term Care Planning and The New Health-Care Law and How it Affects Seniors," there is pleasure seeking language—"providing for your spouse and children"—and pain-avoidance language—"protect your home and assets." Similarly, the ad shown in Figure 21.1 uses pleasure-seeking language—"7 Secrets"—and pain-avoidance language—"make sure your spouse is not left financially ruined if you need nursing home care" and "stay out of the nursing home."

FIGURE 21.1: Ad "7 Secrets You Need to Know"

FREE SEMINAR

The *7 Secrets* You Need To Know...
(to protect your home, your assets, and your family from the costs of long-term care)

Tuesday, October 11th *from* noon – 1:30 p.m.

Lunch included!!!

Location:

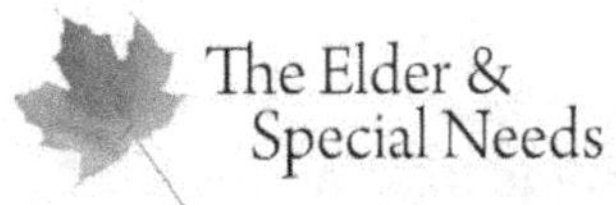

Resource Center

401 Washington Blvd., Williamsport, PA 17701

Nursing home care is more than $94,000 per year!
Attend this *FREE* seminar to learn:

- **How to protect your home and assets from the costs of long-term care**
- **How to stay out of the nursing home and access in-home care**
- **How to make sure your spouse is not left financially ruined if you need nursing home care**
- **How to access Veteran's benefits to pay for long-term care**

Space is limited! Register by Monday October 10.
Please register online at www.steinbacher-stahl.hasaseminarforyou.com
& receive a free audio CD about planning during a health care crisis

Steinbacher & Stahl

Your elder and special needs law firm

Protection

Even though seniors are tight with the purse strings, even with regard to avoiding their own pain, seniors will spend to protect their spouses, children, and grandchildren. What we have repeatedly found with our clients over the past ten years is that husbands want to protect their wives, and women want to protect their children. Some of the "protection" messaging that we have utilized has included the following:

- Protect Your Spouse
- Protect Your Children
- Protect Your Family
- Protect Your Home
- Protect Your Hard-Earned Assets
- Protect Your Life Savings
- Protect Your Estate
- Protect Your Nest Egg
- Protect Your Income
- Protect Your Home from a Lien
- Protect Your Assets from the High Costs of Nursing Home Care
- Preserve Your Legacy

FIGURE 21.2: Ad "Have You Worked Hard . . ."

Have you worked hard for everything you have?
Do you want to protect your assets from
the rising costs of long-term Care?

If you answered yes to either of these questions, then call the law firm with the experience and knowledge to help you:

Nursing home care costs more than $7,900 per month!!

- Protect your home and assets
- Provide for your spouse and children
- Use Veterans benefits to pay for long-term care

You have nothing to lose!

Call our office today to schedule a free consultation.

Also, visit www.Steinbacher-Stahl.protectsyourmoney.com

to claim your coupon for a discount.

Steinbacher & Stahl

Your elder and special needs law firm

413 Washington Blvd., Williamsport, PA 17701

(570) 322-2077

FIGURE 21.3: Ad "Care Crisis Looming?"

Care Crisis Looming?

- A spouse or parent is no longer safe at home
- There is no $ to hire in-home help that would make a difference
- A medical crisis could mean financial ruin
- Want Veterans benefits to pay for assisted living or personal care
- Need to protect assets from the high costs of nursing home care

There is help, there are options, there is a solution...

Without proper planning, 50% of marital assets can be consumed by long-term care costs. Assisted living costs can be over $3,000 per month! Nursing home costs of $7,900 per month will deplete your estate! An estate recovery lien can affect your wishes & your heirs...

Steinbacher & Stahl will help you create a better outcome.

- Explore your long-term care options at a FREE initial consultation
- Protect your home from an estate recovery lien • Protect your assets
- Protect your income • Apply for Veterans benefits
- Find peace of mind at a difficult time

CALL 570-322-2077

Steinbacher & Stahl

Your elder and special needs law firm

413 Washington Blvd., Williamsport, PA 17701
(570) 322-2077

FIGURE 21.4: Ad "Worried About Your Spouse Needing Nursing Home or In-Home Care?"

Worried About Your Spouse Needing Nursing Home or In-Home Care?

Nursing home care costs average $8,000 each month! Without proper planning, 50% of marital assets can be consumed by long-term care costs.

Steinbacher & Stahl will help you:

- Explore your long-term care options at a FREE initial consultation
- Protect your home from an estate recovery lien
- Protect your assets
- Protect your income
- Find peace of mind at a difficult time

Your elder and special needs law firm

413 Washington Blvd., Williamsport • (570) 322-2077
FREE CONSULTATION Home & Hospital Visits
www.sselderlaw.com

We recently used protection and avoidance-of-pain messaging in the title of a book we co-authored with nine other leading lawyers on estate and long-term care planning—***Protect Your Family! Don't Write a Blank Check to the Nursing Home*** (see Figure 21.5).

FIGURE 21.5: Book Cover

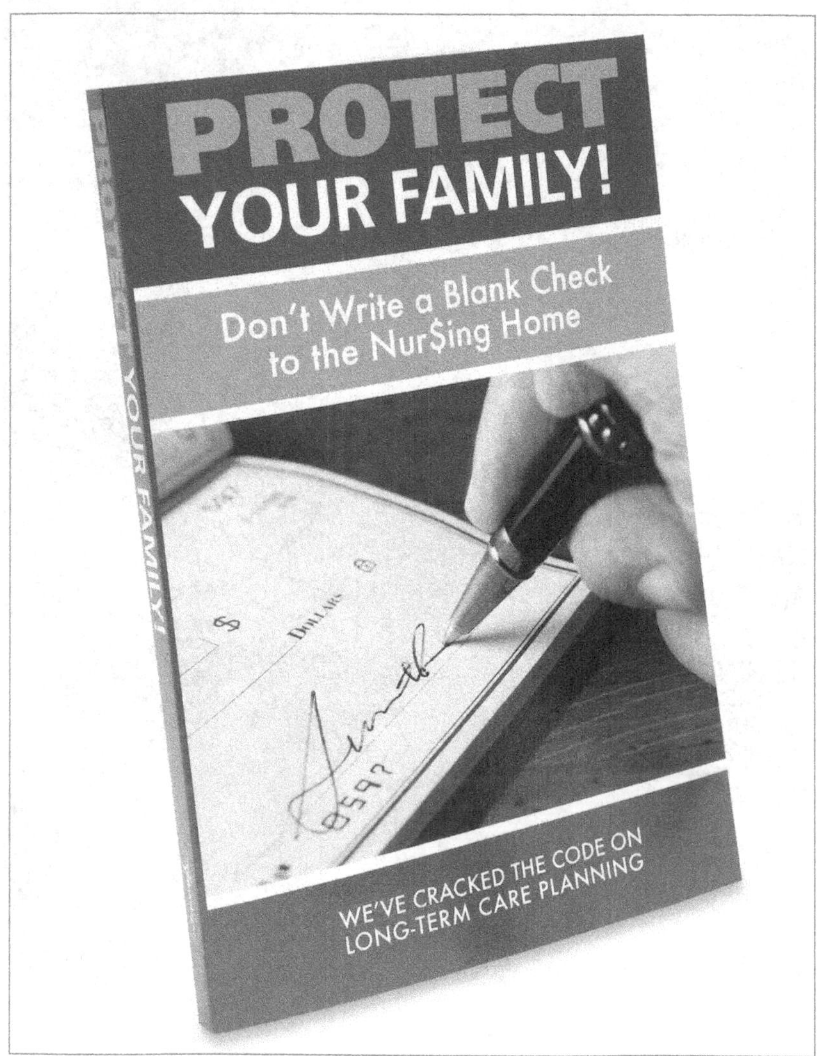

Having lived though the Great Depression, seniors are all too familiar with widespread crisis, and they understand that the government will not protect them. They realize that they must protect themselves and their families, and if they don't realize or have forgotten this, we remind them. We advertised one of our long-term care planning seminars by using the new health-care reform law to get the attention of LEB/S (at that time, President Obama's new health-care act was at the top of the minds of many). Once the LEB/S were at our seminar, we explained that the government's plan to provide for their long-term care needs (the new health-care law) was not going to protect them, their families, or their life savings; and that they needed to take action to protect themselves by planning for their possible long-term care needs (in other words, they needed to hire our firm). See Figure 21.6.

FIGURE 21.6: "Free Seminar on Long-Term Care Planning . . ."

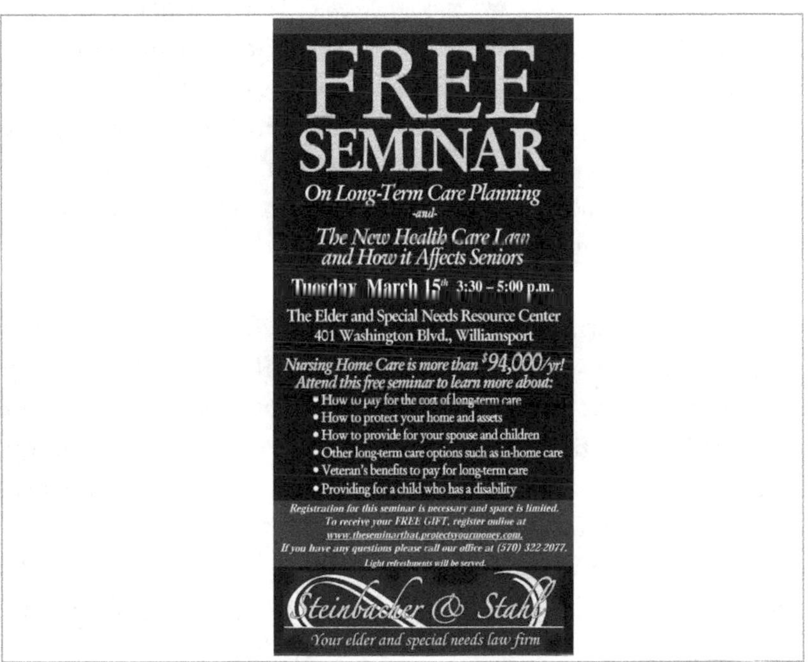

The Power of Credibility and Affinity

Credibility is something else that is important to seniors and aging boomers. For instance, brand names, years in business, and professional affiliations matter more to seniors and aging boomers than to younger consumers. Along those same lines, seniors and aging boomers need to relate to, like, and have affinity with someone before they will buy from that person. In an effort to get our potential clients to begin to relate to, like, and trust us, we ran an ad that had a photo of Julie and said, "**A wife. A mother. A daughter. A social worker. An exceptional elder law attorney.**"

We have authored several books in order to establish ourselves as experts even though the time commitment has been much more than our royalties from the sales. In addition to the book *Protect Your Family! Don't Write a Blank Check to the Nursing Home,* which targets potential clients and referral sources, we have authored two legal books on specific areas of the law, the *Pennsylvania Trust Guide* and the *Pennsylvania Special Needs Planning Guide*.

Additionally, because seniors and aging boomers tend to be skeptical and because the sales process tends to be longer given current economics, seniors and aging boomers respond well to a courtship, per se. Consequently, we established a resource center in a separate building next to our law firm for the purpose of building relationships and helping clients and referral sources to get to know and trust us. Our clients often attend a seminar at our resource center before they engage our services. Likewise, our referral sources often attend a seminar or give a presentation at our resource center before they make a referral to our firm. We've found that spending time, energy, and money to obtain champion referral sources is the best use of our resources because rapport and trust are essentially transferred from the referral source, who is a potential client's trusted advisor, friend, etc., when the trusted person refers a potential client to our firm.

The Power of Nostalgia

We use nostalgia to create an atmosphere that makes LEB/S more likely to buy. Nostalgia is a powerful marketing tool with seniors and boomers, but probably more so with seniors. Selling is always more about the experience and the feelings created than it is about the product or service being sold.

We begin creating a nostalgic effect even before a potential client visits our firm for the first time. After someone schedules an initial consultation with us, we send out a box of decade-appropriate nostalgic candy. We know which decade is relevant because we send the candy after we triage the potential client, finding out his or her age and other relevant information. Candy such as this can be found online at http://www.nostalgiccandy.com/nostalgiccandy.aspx or http://www.oldtimecandy.com/.

Our attempt to create nostalgia continues with the consultation at our office. We purchased a building that was built in the year 1901. We could have purchased a modern office building that would have been less costly up front and in maintenance, but we decided it would be money well spent to be able to capitalize upon the nostalgic influences of the building. The building was built in 1901 as a residence, is in very good condition (we are only the fourth owner), and has its original Tiffany windows. It's rare that a client does not admire the early 1900s arts and crafts style woodwork, trim, and pocket doors, and say, "Boy, they just don't make things like they used to." Subconsciously, our clients give us credit for appreciating the good ol' things and the good ol' days. Our building serves as something of a celebrity—our celebrity endorser!

Care Taken with Language

In marketing to any group, it is important to give thought to what, if any, negative responses your marketing message may elicit from your ideal customer. Traditionally, "elder law" meant working with clients who were in a long-term health-care crisis, who immediately needed nursing home or in-home care, and helping them qualify for public benefits to pay for care and secure placement in a skilled nursing facility or coordinate care in the home. Seniors were the target market for this type of crisis planning, and this planning was often referred to as "nursing home planning" or "Medicaid planning."

Now, elder law has taken on an additional meaning—planning for a long-term care crisis before it strikes. The ideal client in this situation is a 60-year-old healthy person, or better yet, married couple. Because boomers tend to have a fear of getting older, the terminology "elder law" or "nursing home planning" when used in reference to boomers, may elicit negative responses, such as denial or resentment; however, when used in reference to their aging parents, for whom they may be providing care, this terminology is acceptable. In the situation where our ideal client is a healthy person in his or her 60s, we refer to this planning as "long-term care planning" or "senior estate planning" rather than "elder law" or "nursing home planning." In essence, you should give a great deal of consideration to presenting your products and services in a way that avoids triggering negative responses.

Our law firm is successful because of our ability to use protection and avoidance of pain messaging and credibility and nostalgia in marketing to LEB/S. For more information on how to successfully market to LEB/S, visit www.marketing2boomers.com for an incredible FREE gift, *Eleven Essentials to Making Money Marketing to Boomers & Seniors,* which includes a free report, checklist, and video.

CHAPTER 22

Overcoming LEB/S Skeptics and Stress

Ben McClure

As a 33-year-old, selling mattresses to folks more than twice my age can be a challenge. At least on the surface it is. You see, I've got a few things against me. First, nobody truly *enjoys* shopping for a mattress. Second, the industry I'm in is typically not trusted by the general public, especially LEB/S. And third, they see me as a "young man" from a generation that places more value on video games than honor and respect. The deck is stacked against me, right?

I speak to what I know, so I'm going to use my business to show how we overcome objections, but the following principles apply to anyone selling to LEB/S. Take out "mattresses" and replace it with your product or service. OK, here we go . . .

Two things are CRITICAL when marketing and selling to LEB/S:

1. You MUST earn their trust.
2. You MUST overcome their guarded position when they first contact your business.

Obviously, earning someone's trust is imperative before any sale is made, but this is easier said than done when it comes to consumers buying a mattress. Typically, LEB/S entering our store haven't bought a new bed in a long time. Some, in a VERY long time. Much has changed in the bedding industry since their last purchase and the process can be completely overwhelming. So what do we do?

It was obvious to us that we needed to become the consumer advocate for LEB/S in the bedding industry. Our book, which makes us the trusted authority in our market, addresses common mattress-buying mistakes and shows our customers how to avoid them. Available for download from our website (which LEB/S use more than you think!), it immediately puts them at ease to know that they have found a store more interested in education than the typical "half off—buy it today sale." The education the book provides allows our boomer customers to feel comfortable and confident when they enter our showroom, instead of timid and wary. This makes a huge difference in our closing ratio. A book is not all that difficult to write; simply take what you know about your product or service and put it to paper. Our book can be found on our website www.GardnersMattressAndMore.com or www.LancasterSleepExperts.com.

Another way to earn a LEB/S's trust is to provide an experience they will not find with any of your competition. At Gardner's, our unique selling proposition is our Dream Room. The Dream Room is a private mattress-testing room, designed to allow a prospective buyer the proper time to "Try Before They Buy" any mattress in our showroom. The Dream Room is especially attractive to LEB/S because of their changing physical sleep needs. As their body changes, they need to spend the proper time making the right decision. Through the use of the room, our customers are guaranteed, in writing, that the investment in their mattress will best suit their sleep needs or we will exchange it for the one that does. There is no other retailer in our market offering such a service, and our conversion ratio is 98% when someone uses the room. What is your "Dream Room"?

Another strategy for building trust with our LEB/S customers is to ask our happy customers to speak for us. Our referral system not only allows us to reduce our advertising budget on costly media, it brings a prospect into the store who already knows about our excellent service. A referral program can work in many ways; ours has two main tiers. First, we introduce our referral program at the point of sale and tell them about the 5% cash reward for their referral (of referral's purchase). Then, we follow up with a thank-you card after delivery reminding them of the referral reward. The second tier of the referral program rewards with points rather than cash. Points can then be traded in for gift cards to local retailers and restaurants, experience-based gifts like golf packages, and even vacations. Seventy-five percent of the time, the referred prospect buys on their first visit to the store due to the already established trust built by the referring customer, compared to the norm of 50%.

Another point of differentiation is in our print media advertising. Not to say the LEB/S don't use the internet, but we find that print material is their first choice of media. See our examples included in Figures 22.1 to 22.5 of this chapter, and refer to our website. Notice a few things that are missing? I'll give you the answer—prices, "LOUD" promotional gimmicks, specifications, and warranties. Every other competitor in our marketplace promotes themselves in this fashion, and only contributes to the confusion highlighted earlier. Give the LEB/S a different reason to look into you and they will. Our newspaper advertisements (4:1 return on investment) and advertorials (7:1) are focused on our customers and the benefits, not features, (note the difference) gained by doing business with us. When they do go to the website the message is consistent. Imagine if they were greeted on our homepage with the typical "yakety yak" sales gimmicks done by everyone else? They would immediately bounce off the homepage. When we switched the focus to 100% benefit-driven information we noticed a huge impact in two categories. Time on our site increased by 25%, and visits to our site increased by 30%—a direct result due to the amount of relevant information we are now providing.

Our advertorials are placed in the dominant magazine for our marketplace, *Fine Living Lancaster.* By design and place strategy we're attracting LEB/S with money to spend, as opposed to those pinching each penny just hoping to make it all the way to the end without having to hand out shopping carts at Walmart just to get by in retirement. Our advertorials tell stories, which we all love and people mostly relate to. Plus it gives our customers something to talk to us about and puts a human element in the shopping experience as opposed to, "I'm here for the big sale."

Lastly, as everyone else in our niche is vacating one of the last tried-and-true places to find LEB/S, the Yellow Pages, we are embracing it. And winning, BIG. Another example of place strategy shows that being where everyone else *isn't* is resulting in great ROI. (Some months as high as 15:1 ROI; average month 7:1 ROI). See the example of our Yellow Pages ad found in the chiropractic section (Figure 22.5) of our local book. We are the only mattress store here and we even highjack the listing with our headline of "25,000 chiropractors endorse Tempur-Pedic®." Two strategies are here, really: implied endorsement, the headline, and use of celebrity, by using Tempur-Pedic's name. Where and how can you employ this same place strategy?

So now we've gained LEB/S trust, what else might we have to overcome? LEB/S, more than any other generation of customers, seem to have a very guarded position when it comes to shopping for a mattress. Perhaps, and very likely, they have had a prior buying experience that was not a good one. Also, it's highly probable that their current mattress (and others preceding it) have not lived up to expectations. Lastly, they are confused by the myriad of brand and price advertising designed exactly for that purpose by the majority of our competitive retailers. Fortunately, our unique sales process to custom fit a new mattress to their body's individual sleep needs addresses these factors.

With LEB/S, we have a unique opportunity to increase our average ticket, sometimes doubling the sale. They tend to have more issues affecting their sleep, warranting the need for a bed that customizes to those changing sleep needs. A power adjustable bed elevates the head and legs into a more comfortable position to reduce the effects of snoring, reflux, back/hip/knee pain, circulation trouble, fibromyalgia, and restless leg syndrome, to name a few. I bring this up because it is a great opportunity for us to provide our customer with a bed they not only need but love, AND nearly doubles our sale.

It's worth asking: What upgraded or enhanced version of your product(s) or service(s) could be found or developed and offered that best suits the special needs of LEB/S and gives you a higher dollar sale or profit per customer?

Ben McClure and his partner, Jeff Giagnocavo, are the proprietors of www.GardnersMattressAndMore.com, the main store in Lancaster, Pennsylvania, and are in the development stage of national franchise expansion to key markets with affluent LEB/S population density. They can be reached via the website or by phone at (717) 299-6228.

FIGURE 22.1: Gardner Mattress Book Cover

FIGURE 22.2: View of Book Pages

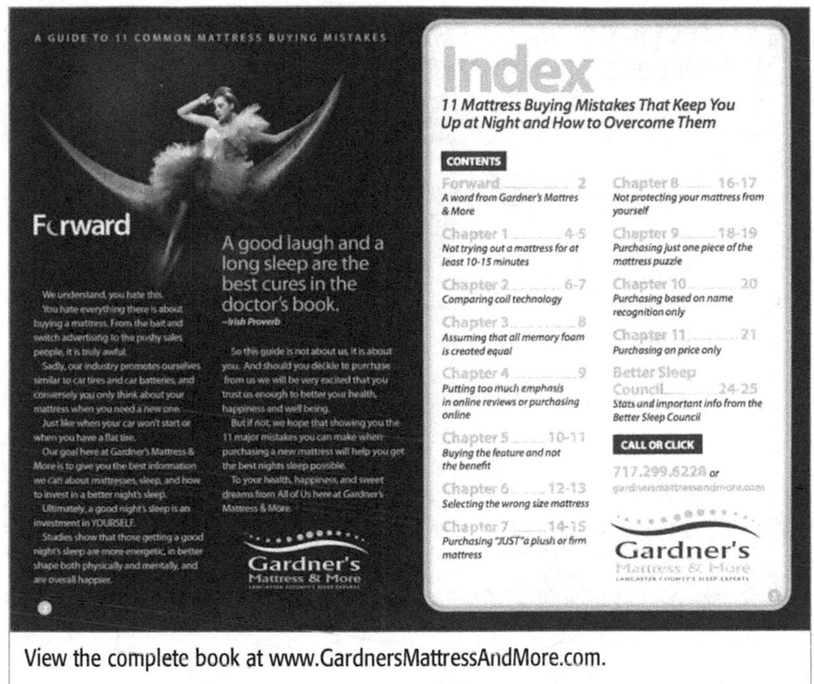

A GUIDE TO 11 COMMON MATTRESS BUYING MISTAKES

Forward

We understand, you hate this.

You hate everything there is about buying a mattress. From the bait and switch advertising to the pushy sales people, it is truly awful.

Sadly, our industry promotes ourselves similar to car tires and car batteries, and conversely you only think about your mattress when you need a new one.

Just like when your car won't start or when you have a flat tire.

Our goal here at Gardner's Mattress & More is to give you the best information we can about mattresses, sleep, and how to invest in a better night's sleep.

Ultimately, a good night's sleep is an investment in YOURSELF.

Studies show that those getting a good night's sleep are more energetic, in better shape both physically and mentally, and are overall happier.

A good laugh and a long sleep are the best cures in the doctor's book.
~Irish Proverb

So this guide is not about us, it is about you. And should you decide to purchase from us we will be very excited that you trust us enough to better your health, happiness and well being.

But if not, we hope that showing you the 11 major mistakes you can make when purchasing a new mattress will help you get the best nights sleep possible.

To your health, happiness, and sweet dreams from All of Us here at Gardner's Mattress & More.

Gardner's
Mattress & More

Index

11 Mattress Buying Mistakes That Keep You Up at Night and How to Overcome Them

CONTENTS

CALL OR CLICK

717.299.6228 or gardnersmattressandmore.com

Gardner's
Mattress & More
LANCASTER COUNTY'S SLEEP EXPERTS

View the complete book at www.GardnersMattressAndMore.com.

FIGURE 22.3: Not Your Typical Display

FIGURE 22.4: Advertorial Placed as a Magazine Advertisement

The Secrets of The Satisfied Sleepers

By Ben McClure

They all laughed at me when I told them my bed moves up and down. But when I get up in the morning, well before anyone else, they all ask, "How does he do it?"

My friends all said, "Wow Ben, isn't a hospital bed for old people? What do you need the head and foot to move for? Nerd." Yep, that's me—sleep nerd. But is that really a bad thing? I care about my sleep and I have the best possible sleep system in my bedroom. Sure, my bed goes up and down, but that doesn't make me old and it doesn't mean I'm ill. It means I can customize my comfort to find the position that best suits my sleep needs. When I go to sleep, no matter how my body feels, my bed can adjust to me; I don't have to adjust to it. Very cool. I can even control my bed from my iPhone! Dork. But enough about me.

My passion for better sleep doesn't stop with my bedroom. I care about your sleep as well, and I'm passionate about helping my customers get the most out of their mattress every night, and wake up each morning feeling the best that they can. Let's face it, our day-to-day routines are rough on our bodies. Whether it's heavy lifting at work, being on your feet all day long, working on the endless list of household chores, or hauling the kids in and out of the van ten times a day, it takes a huge physical toll on our bodies. Some days you use muscles you didn't even know you had. And we've all had that nagging pain that takes days to go away. Your body needs a break at night. Your muscles need to relax, and your joints need to rest. Think about your current mattress. Do you feel refreshed in the morning?

Imagine being able to lie down in bed and have the bed adjust to you; move for you; feel amazing. All for you. Power adjustable sleep systems do what no other bed can do. Customizable support and comfort help you fall asleep quickly and stay sleeping throughout the night. When paired with the proper mattress, power adjustable sleep systems can do things most ordinary mattresses can only dream about. A power sleep system can adjust your body to a zero gravity position to improve circulation and reduce lower back discomfort. Power beds typically include massage vibration therapy to relax muscles. Like to read or watch television in bed? Adjust your bed into a comfortable elevated position instead of getting frustrated with shifting pillows. Some advanced power sleep systems include benefits such as a built-in clock with a massage wake-up alarm, in case you are prone to over-sleeping. There is even a base with a "snore-stop" function for someone who saws wood all night long!

Of course power sleep systems can aid numerous health issues. Raise your hand if you suffer from something on this list: back pain, leg, neck and shoulder pain, acid reflux and gastroesophageal reflux disease, hiatal hernia, poor circulation, sleep apnea, snoring, mobility issues, breathing restrictions, restless leg syndrome, or fibromyalgia. If you raised your hand, maybe you're the nerd. Just kidding. But seriously, it would be hard to find someone who didn't suffer from something on this list. I personally have difficulty breathing when I lay flat and also deal with some reflux issues. Being able to elevate my head slightly greatly reduces those issues. So naturally, my bed is not only great for me right now, but will continue to be a blessing as my body ages and other sleep needs arise.

As if it's not bad enough having my friends laugh at me, they fell on the floor when I told that about my investment in the other half of my sleep system, my Tempur-Pedic mattress. My reply was very simple and to the point. The investment in myself pays me dividends with increased energy, focus, and overall just plain feeling better. Tempur-Pedic mattresses offer a great amount of pressure point reduction and limited tossing and turning with their exclusive Tempur material. I figure I gain at least an extra hour of productivity each day as a result of my mattress and sleep system. At the end of the year this amounts to 365 hours. That is a little over two solid weeks worth of extra time that is a part of my life. My friends, of course, are having the energy sucked out of them on their $399 special purchase, once in a lifetime, this week only, 50% off friends and family, close-out, limited time only, special purchase, super spectacular mattress.

With all that I get out of my sleep system, it is really silly to me that a grown person wouldn't want to invest in themselves, in something they do for a third of their life! Maybe it is because most don't like mattress shopping. Or maybe it is because most mattress stores follow a strict policy of "pumping and dumping" their customers into the most expensive mattress as fast as they can. Maybe it is the fact that you just need a place to truly try out a mattress in private without the pressure of a pushy salesperson. Well, and promise not to laugh at the obvious plug, my store Gardner's Mattress & More is the place that answers all of these common issues when looking to invest in a great night's sleep. I wrote a book to help you avoid common mattress buying mistakes. I also developed, by all accounts, the only place on the eastern seaboard to try out a sleep system in private in our exclusive "Dream Room." We are the only store that will allow you to select a mattress and try it out before you buy in our private mattress testing "Dream Room." You can see a video of this room on our website at www.GardnersMattressAndMore.com. If you would like to get a copy of my book, please stop in at our store or go to www.LancasterSleepExperts.com to get a free e-book download.

Gardner's Mattress & More (formerly Gardner's Bedrooms) is pleased to announce their Grand Opening through the end of this month. Furthering a 20-year tradition in Lancaster County, Ben McClure is excited to present his vision of a true sleep system mattress store. Complete with all types of mattresses, power sleep systems, platform beds, storage beds, and kids' furniture, Gardner's Mattress & More is truly the place to invest in your sleep.

Slumber

CONTENT PROVIDED BY:

Gardner's
Mattress & More

Gardner's Mattress & More
830 Plaza Blvd Ste. 2
Lancaster PA 17601
717.299.6228
www.GardnersMattressAndMore.com

Ben McClure, owner, has been helping Lancaster County residents improve their sleep for the past 11 years. Gardner's Mattress & More has been Lancaster County's headquarters for premium mattress products and sound sleep advice since 1990. Gardner's has Lancaster County's largest Adjustable Power Bed display and has been an authorized Tempur-Pedic dealer since 2001.

23

FIGURE 22.5: "Out of Category" Yellow Pages Ad

yellowbook™ **COPY SHEET** AD LETTER ☐ Replaces Previous Copy

Hate Mattress Shopping?

Make It Easy! Get Our Free Book, at LancasterSleepExperts.com or in our store!

TEMPUR-PEDIC

iComfort

Lancaster's Favorite Mattress Store!

Call Us Today 717-299-6228

830 Plaza Blvd Lancaster, Behind The Park City Mall

GardnersMattressAndMore.com

Mattress Sets From $199 To $19,999!

Bedrooms From Infant To Adult And More!

Gardner's
Mattress & More
LANCASTER COUNTY'S SLEEP EXPERTS

I Approve This Copy. Cust. Sign.: X ______________ Sales Rep.: Brian C. Hickey 18636 Date: ________

Please note - quality and size may vary slightly between proof and actual directory

SECTION 4

RESOURCES

About the Authors

Dan S. Kennedy is a multimillionaire serial entrepreneur, strategic advisor, and marketing consultant, one of the highest paid direct-response copywriters in America, a popular speaker for association and corporate groups, and a prolific author and editor of seven different monthly newsletters. He is on the Advisory Board of the School of Communications at High Point University, the Board of Trustees of the Media Research Center, a frequent contributor to www.BusinessAndMedia.org, and a founder of the Information Marketing Association. He has been a celebrated thought leader in the field of marketing for more than three decades, and he has been intimately involved in epic marketing success stories involving virtually every media including print, direct mail, direct-response radio and TV, TV infomercials, and online media, often engineering million-dollar to multimillion-dollar improvements to clients' marketing campaigns, multimillion-dollar product launches almost overnight, and brokering relationships between clients creating new opportunities. He has assisted one of the fastest growth franchisors of recent history; a company grown from startup to nearly $2 billion by direct marketing; one of the fastest growing small-business software companies; and networks of restaurants, service businesses, health-care practices, and financial advisory practices numbering in the thousands. He frequently assists clients with obtaining celebrities for marketing campaigns, development of multimedia marketing systems, and development of authority marketing tools such as books, video presentations, and newsletters. As a speaker, Mr. Kennedy has repeatedly shared the platform with four former U.S. Presidents, with business leaders, celebrity entrepreneurs, media personalities, and all the top business and marketing experts, addressing audiences from 1,000 to 35,000, in over 2,000 compensated appearances.

To communicate with Mr. Kennedy directly about his availability for speaking, development and presentation of customized speeches, seminars, or corporate training programs and mastermind meetings, consulting, copywriting or co-authorship, please fax your request to (602) 269-3113, write to 15433 N. Tatum Blvd. #104, Phoenix, AZ 85032, or phone (602) 997-7707. Mr. Kennedy famously does not use email or other online communication. Do NOT communicate with him via the internet.

For information about his books, his newsletters, and resources published by GKIC, and GKIC Conferences:

www.NoBSBooks.com
www.DanKennedy.com

CHIP KESSLER is an entrepreneur, the leading marketing and business development consultant and staff training publisher to the nursing-home, assisted-living and in-home health care fields, and an advisor to other health care businesses. He is also co-author with Dan Kennedy of one of the most unusual marketing books ever published, *Making Them Believe: The 21 Principles and Lost Secrets of Dr. J.R. Brinkley-Style Marketing,* featuring the promoter of one of the very first "cures" for erectile dysfunction, at the turn of the century. Chip is available for speaking engagements and consulting assignments. His business information can be obtained at:

www.ExtendedCareProducts.com
www.ChoicesForCare.com
www.ChipKessler.com

Other Books by the Authors

By Dan Kennedy, in the No B.S. Series, published by Entrepreneur Press:

No B.S. Grassroots Marketing for Local Businesses (with Jeff Slutsky)
No B.S. Trust-Based Marketing (with Matt Zagula)
No B.S. Price Strategy (with Jason Marrs)
No B.S. Marketing to the Affluent
No B.S. Business Success in The New Economy
No B.S. Sales Success in The New Economy
No B.S. Wealth Attraction in The New Economy
No B.S. Ruthless Management of People and Profits
No B.S. Direct Marketing for Non-Direct Marketing Businesses
No B.S. Time Management for Entrepreneurs

Other books by Dan Kennedy

Ultimate Marketing Plan (4th/20th Anniversary Edition), Adams Media

Ultimate Sales Letter (4th/20th Anniversary Edition), Adams Media

Uncensored Sales Strategies with Sydney Barrows, Entrepreneur Press

The New Psycho-Cybernetics with Dr. Maxwell Maltz, Prentice-Hall

Unfinished Business/Autobiographical Essays, Advantage

Make 'em Laugh & Take Their Money, GKIC/Morgan-James

By Dan Kennedy and Chip Kessler

Making Them Believe: The 21 Principles and Lost Secrets of Dr. Brinkley-Style Marketing, GKIC/Morgan-James

Special Guest Contributors

1. Jeff Giagnocavo and Ben McClure, Gardner's Mattress, www.GardnersMattressAndMore.com
2. Dean Killingbeck, www.NewCustomersNowMarketing.com
3. Dr. Charles Martin, DDS, www.MasterYourPractice.com
4. Julieanne E. Steinbacher and Adrianne J. Stahl, Attorneys at Law, www.Marketing2Boomers.com

Sources and Resources

Experts in Marketing to Boomers and Seniors

Dr. Ken Dychtwald
Age Wave
www.AgeWave.com

Ken is a psychologist, gerontologist, and entrepreneur who has been studying the transformative power of demographic forces and doing groundbreaking research since 1973. Age Wave is his think tank and advisory group, guiding Fortune 500 companies and government groups in marketing to and serving boomers and mature adults. He has appeared as an expert on age-wave trends on CNN, ABC News, and countless other media outlets. Age Wave often conducts commissioned research studies for corporate clients, subsequently used in public relations initiatives by those clients. The Age Wave Group provides expert speakers to associations, organizations and corporations.

Mary Furlong
Mary Furlong & Associates
www.MaryFurlong.com

Founded in 2003, Furlong & Associates delivers strategy, business development, and public relations services to corporate clients marketing to boomers. Sponsors the annual What's Next: Boomer Business Summit and the Boomer Ventures Summit. Mary has appeared on CBS, NBC, PBS, and NPR and been featured in *Business Week, Fortune,* and *Fast Company* as an authority on boomers. Before launching MFA, Mary founded the nonprofit SeniorNet and Third Age Media, creating membership rolls exceeding two million. Throughout the course of her work for these organizations she raised $120 million in venture capital, corporate sponsorships, and foundation grants.

The Boomer Project
www.BoomerProject.com

The Boomer Project is a research and strategy company, advising businesses on the 50-and-older market. Its CEO, John W. Martin, and its founder, Matt Thornhill, co-authored the book, *The Boomer Consumer.* Matt has appeared on NBC, CBS, and CNBC and quoted in *The Wall Street Journal* as an expert on boomer behavior.

Matt Zagula
Z-K Marketing Consultants
www.MattZagula.com

Matt Zagula is a leading financial advisor with two thriving practices, one in association with four-time Super Bowl champion Rocky Bleier. His in-industry consultancy and marketing company works with high-income financial advisors nationwide, specializing in retirement planning, guaranteed lifetime income planning, and other issues of importance to boomers and seniors. He is the author of *Invasion of the Money Snatchers* (for retirees) and co-author with Dan Kennedy of *No B.S. Guide to Trust-Based Marketing*. Together, Zagula and Kennedy have developed proprietary advertising, marketing, and client educational materials, workshop marketing, lead generation systems, and book and client newsletter publishing program for exclusive use by select financial advisors.

Jim Gilmartin
Coming of Age, Inc.
www.ComingofAge.com

A full-service online (digital) and traditional marketing advertising, PR, and sales and service training firm specializing in helping clients to capture and keep LEB/S customers.

Other Important Expert Resources

Harry Dent Jr. & Associates
www.HSDent.com

Publisher of the *Boom or Bust* financial newsletter, a leading research and consulting organization focused on "demographics as destiny" for development of business, investment, product innovation, and marketing strategy. Harry Dent, Jr., is available for speaking engagements. His newest book is *The Great Crash Ahead.*

Craig Simpson
www.Simpson-Direct.com

Direct-mail marketing project management, including list research, selection and procurement, coordinating copywriters, graphic artists, production, printing, and mailing.

Fred Catona
Bulldozer Digital
www.bulldozerdigital.com
1-800-652-3837

Direct-response radio project management, including creative consulting, script writing, test marketing, station/network selection, media buying, and analysis.

Publications and Websites

AARP Study, December, 2010: "Approaching 65: A Survey of Baby Boomers Turning 65 Years Old," www.aarp.org/research

Business and Media Institute, www.BusinessAndMedia.org

2010 Del Webb Baby Boomer Survey, www.dwboomersurvey.com

Ipsos Mendelsohn, "Affluent Generations Survey," www.Ipsos.com

L2 Think Tank for Digital Innovation, www.L2ThinkTank.com

Media Research Center, www.MRC.org

Nation's Restaurant News, www.NRN.com

No B.S. Marketing Letter and *No B.S. Marketing to the Affluent Letter*, www.DanKennedy.com

Research Alert–the definitive source for consolidated research on consumer spending, behavior and attitudes. EPM Communications, www.epmcom.com

U.S. Department of Labor, U.S. Census Bureau, www.dol.gov, www.census.gov

Books Specific to Marketing to LEB/S

Turning Silver into Gold: How to Profit in the New Boomer Marketplace, Dr. Mary Furlong

The Boomer Consumer: Ten New Rules for Marketing to America's Largest, Wealthiest, Most Influential Group by Thornhill and Martin

AgePower: How The 21st Century Will Be Ruled by the New Old by Dr. Ken Dychtwald

Marketing to the Mindset of Boomers and Their Elders by Carol M. Morgan and Doran J. Levy

BOOM: Marketing to the Ultimate Power Consumer, The Baby-Boomer Woman by Mary Brown and Carol Orsborn

Books—General Marketing

Buy•ology: Truth & Lies About Why We Buy by Martin Lindstrom

Meaningful Marketing by Doug Hall

The Purpose Driven Church by Pastor Rick Warren

Psychology of Influence by Dr. Robert Cialdini

The Culture Code by Clotaire Rapaille

Fascinate by Sally Hogshead

Index

S

T